I Lift Up
My Eyes
To the Hills

Albert Camus wrote about his dual commitment to be faithful to the oppressed *and* faithful to beauty. This book seeks to be faithful to both in a moving series of personal stories that discover beauty and grace in the midst of poverty. It is also a living testimony to the biblical truth that "it is in giving that we receive."

DOUGLAS W. OLDENBURG
President, Columbia Seminary
Decatur, Georgia

With a listening ear and a compassionate heart, Nancy Dawe offers compelling stories from the hills and hollows of Appalachia.

DAVID DOUGLAS
Author of *Wilderness Sojourn*

Moving, sensitive, and thoroughly captivating . . . A celebration of mutual giving and receiving that renews the human spirit. Nancy Dawe's writing is as honest and spare as the people in her stories, and her experiences as rugged and beautiful as the mountains where she worked.

The Rev. JERRY K. ROBBINS
Morgantown, West Virginia

I Lift Up My Eyes To the Hills

Stories of Faith and Joy from Appalachia

Text and photographs by NANCY ANNE DAWE

Design by Linda Crittenden

Augsburg
MINNEAPOLIS

To the great, good God who provided this feast;
and to the Reverend Bob Bondurant and his wife,
Beth, who invited us all to God's table.

I LIFT UP MY EYES TO THE HILLS
Stories of Faith and Joy from Appalachia

Copyright © 1992 Augsburg Fortress. All rights reserved. Except for brief quotations in critical articles or reviews, no part of this book may be reproduced in any manner without prior written permission from the publisher. Write to: Permissions, Augsburg Fortress, 426 S. Fifth St., Box 1209, Minneapolis, MN 55440.

Scripture quotations unless otherwise noted are from the New Revised Standard Version of the Bible, copyright © 1989 by the Division of Christian Education of the National Council of the Churches of Christ in the United States of America.

ON THE COVER West Virginian Mae Snyder was 82 when she was photographed in 1981. This sturdy Appalachian still tilled her own garden, and sheltered stray animals who came her way.

Photograph on Page 7 by Don Dawe.
Photograph on page 106 by Paul Barber.

Library of Congress Cataloging-in-Publication Data
Dawe, Nancy Anne,
    I lift up my eyes to the hills : stories of faith and joy from Appalachia / text and photographs by Nancy Anne Dawe : design by Linda Crittenden.
      p. cm.
    ISBN 0-8066-2596-1 (acid-free paper)
    1. Work camps—West Virginia. 2. West Virginia—Religious life and customs. 3. Dawe, Nancy Anne,
1931-   . I. Title.
BV1650.D39 1992   91-38070
277.54′0827—dc20   CIP

The paper used in this publication meets the minimum requirements of American National Standard for Information Sciences—Permanence of Paper for Printed Library Materials, ANSI Z329.48-1984. ∞™

Manufactured in the U.S.A.   AF 9-2596

96   95   94   93   92   1   2   3   4   5   6   7   8   9   10

PREFACE

When I set out from my Massachusetts seaside home in June 1975 for my first ecumenical work camp in the Appalachian Mountains of West Virginia, I had no idea that eighteen years later I would still be journeying there. Not even an intervening move to Atlanta would stop these annual trips, for something profound had transpired during that initial two-week stay.

When Presbyterian minister Bob Bondurant founded the work camp in his rural, West Virginia county in 1968, he could not have predicted that twenty-four years later it would still be going strong. Nor could he have envisioned that through those years, over 2,000 volunteers would come from seventeen states, four foreign countries, and twelve denominations to repair and rebuild over one thousand homes of the aged, sick, and needy.

Although I had traveled widely and had many exciting adventures, nothing, except family, drew me like Appalachia. Here, where life was stripped to simplicities, I was to find the most sublime experiences of my life and learn the truth of Matthew 18:20: "Where two or three are gathered in my name, I am there among them." NANCY ANNE DAWE

CONTENTS

To walk a holler was to be enthralled: daisies
and clover in piquant parade; a farmer and
wife, pitchforks in hand, turning hay in a far-
off field; calves and cows that lifted languid
eyes to watch me as I passed.

1

My Appalachia

**I lift up my
eyes to the hills—**
PSALM 121:1

Welcome to Wild, Wonderful West Virginia, the sign said as our caravan of adults and teens crossed the state line. We had left our Massachusetts town the morning before, bound for an ecumenical work camp deep in the Appalachian Mountains. I was also on my way, although I didn't know it then, to a lasting love affair with Appalachia.

The county to which we were heading was 93 percent forested with rich stands of pine and poplar, beneath which lay wide seams of bituminous coal. But amid these abundant resources, hidden in "hollers," on mountainsides, even tucked in towns, were pockets of poverty.

The work camps had been founded "to show what Christ's church might be like," with the practical goal of making every home in the county warm, safe, and dry. Each June, volunteers from many states came to donate two weeks' work. We had educated ourselves before setting out, reading Appalachian history, hearing bluegrass tunes, corresponding with people from previous camps. And we had

Our ears popping from pressure, we ascended the steepening hills, passing barns painted with Chew Mail Pouch Tobacco, railroad sidings lined with coal cars, crystal creeks, cascading streams.

learned about some hazards: "Don't put your hands where your eyes can't see. Mountains have copperheads and rattlers." But nothing truly prepared us for the powerful panorama soon to penetrate our hearts.

Our ears popping from pressure, we ascended the steepening hills, passing barns painted with Chew Mail Pouch Tobacco, railroad sidings lined with coal cars, crystal creeks, cascading streams. There were no shopping malls, no subdivisions, no traffic—only rustic houses, some tidy, others with cluttered yards.

Nearing our destination, we entered the

county seat, faintly reminiscent of a frontier town, its old men sitting by a sulfur-water well. Then we circled up a final mountain, where cloud shadows rippled like great sea waves over verdant, rolling terrain.

How wild it had all seemed—that first sight of "my" Appalachia!

The days ahead were filled with hard work as we nailed, painted, roofed, and dug. But they also held sheer, surprising joy. We swirled at a square dance with a hillbilly caller: "Come on! Grab a girl. She won't bite!" And we downed hamburgers at the Humdinger toward the end of day. There were swims in the

There were no shopping malls, no subdivisions, no traffic—only rustic houses, some tidy, others with cluttered yards.

Nothing truly prepared us for the powerful panorama soon to penetrate our hearts.

Williams River and tumbles from a Tarzan rope into waters of beautiful Blue Hole. We explored the Back Fork of the Elk River to see the big sycamore and picnicked in the peaceful shade by shining Sugar Creek.

And we learned to appreciate the people and the land.

Before that initial work camp trip, Appalachia to me meant poverty; and poverty is what I saw at first—some of it intense. But returning to camp each succeeding year, my focus changed until poverty became the least of it. For Appalachia revealed its experience: I descended into coal mines and learned most miners love their work; watched rough logs enter lumber mills to emerge as smooth, sweet-smelling planks; and discovered that the lovely landscape was inhabited by people of integrity and grace.

One June, we tar papered the roof of Warder and Rosie Johns's place, way out on Missouri Run. Rosie, fifty-nine, looked a great deal older; Warder, seventy-six, had a bad heart. But once he had worked the mines, logged the woods, and "toiled on the railroad five year and a half." Like many Appalachian women, Rosie had spent her life surviving: "warshing down walls" to earn money for her

Before that initial work camp trip, Appalachia to me meant poverty; and poverty is what I saw at first—some of it intense. But returning to camp each succeeding year, my focus changed until poverty became the least of it. For Appalachia revealed its experience.

We explored the Back Fork of the Elk River to see the big sycamore and picnicked in the peaceful shade by shining Sugar Creek.

drapes; cooking milkweed stems like green beans "when things was kinder hard"; passing her time hoeing, canning, tending kin.

Short and thin yet sturdy, she was thoughtful and generous, offering blackberry cobbler, cool water from the well, and a quilt top she had sewn from old cotton frocks.

Rosie was also savvy and shrewd, despite an education aborted "after three years in second grade." When a neighbor's calf "was ailing from too much milk," she had cured it by digging and boiling yellowroot and pouring the potion down its throat. She was equally adept at protecting herself, whisking a loaded .38 from under a chest while pointing to four loaded rifles over her bed.

From other Appalachians, I learned the lore, like that of old, one-legged Sherman McAllister. "My granddaddy was waylaid and killed on Miller Mountain, and I seen the devil in the woods m'self. Would 'a shot him, too, but missed." There were tales of the murderer who'd escaped scot-free, whose mattress had burst into flames at his death. There were stories of the haunted house at the end of a holler, where a little girl's ghost appeared on the porch.

The mountains held other mysteries, too: an effigy hanging from a leafy branch along a rough and lonely road; and the "Woman Who Stood" in a daily trance, awaiting the son unreturned from a war.

To walk a holler was to be enthralled: daisies and clover in piquant parade; a farmer and wife, pitchforks in hand, turning hay in a far-off field; calves, colts, piglets, chicks, and cows that lifted languid eyes to watch me as I passed. I saw snakes aplenty, too, and groundhogs and deer, and I knew the higher elevations sheltered lynx and bear.

The mountains held other mysteries, too: an effigy hanging from a leafy branch along a rough and lonely road; and the "Woman Who Stood" in a daily trance, awaiting the son unreturned from a war.

If we had come to Appalachia thinking we'd do great things for others, instead we were the ones who had changed. For in living among people sustained by fundamentals, we rediscovered the essentials ourselves.

I saw the sun rise at Point Mountain and sink scarlet behind the steep, black hills. And one year toward the close of camp, wanting to photograph the setting sun, I drove out to Big Ditch Lake. Arriving early, I sat on a slope, enveloped in a sense of peace.

I zeroed in with my telephoto lens on some chattering, silhouetted birds. After socializing in the reeds a while, they lifted in flight, only to circle back and land again. My annual return to Appalachia was much the same, and the ripples on the water turned to silver as I mused on the reasons why.

I knew that despite our mobile world, traditions still existed here. On the side of the lake that paralleled the road, a group of old men fished. Directly across from the men, a grandmother and grandson sat shoulder to shoulder, their lines simultaneously cast. A teenager sat on lakeside rocks, the golden sun lighting his face. Whole families were there.

There was simplicity as well, like the potter

I saw at a fair one year, his fluid hands shaping vases on his wheel, and the foot-stomping tunes that played their way off a fiddler's violin.

I was thrilled at the stunning beauty, too, of night's black pastures alight with fireflies— then sunrise turning dew-dropped grasses into fields of morning jewels.

But I had also seen pain and dignity in the midst of deprivation. If we had come to Appalachia thinking we'd do great things for others, instead we were the ones who had changed. For in living among people sustained by fundamentals, we rediscovered the essentials ourselves.

I travel to work camp from Atlanta now, drawn by the same simple ties. Wild and wonderful is "my" Appalachia, its riches as real as the heart.

I was thrilled at the stunning beauty, too, of night's black pastures alight with fireflies—then sunrise turning dew-dropped grasses into fields of morning jewels.

Now here I was in steep, stunning mountains. . . . And deep among them I found three Appalachian women— and many men and women after that— who would change my life forever.

2

Three Appalachian Women

Bouncing one hundred miles over the mountains one bright June day in 1975, helping Bob Bondurant deliver work camp supplies, I thought back to events that had brought me there.

The January before, I had eagerly signed up for work camp, part of our town's continuing commitment to a beloved Catholic priest, Father Ken. While in Massachusetts, he had not only served his own church, but, deeply involved in the town's ecumenical movement, he had served on the staffs of two Protestant churches as well. When subsequently called to Appalachia, he had left many friends behind, and it seemed natural that when he joined work camp, we would attend, too.

That January, Father Ken had visited town, accompanied by the work camp's founder, a Presbyterian minister, the Reverend Bob Bondurant. A stranger to us at the time, he spoke eloquently at an ecumenical church meeting.

"Ours is a beautiful county," he began.

"There are places in West Virginia where you come down between hills, all the houses are together, and there's dirt, soot, and coal mines. But we're at a high elevation, with glades something like your cranberry bogs. There's clean air, about 10,000 people, and one highway running the county's length.

"There are problems, though, because everybody doesn't live right on the highway, and when you go up the 'hollers,' and sometimes right in our communities, you see some distressing things—some unknown even to my parishioners.

"I went to one house a couple of years ago before work camp had begun that year to ask if they needed help. The door was broken, window glass was missing, and it was still cool . . . April. The lady said, 'I'd appreciate it if you could fix my windows and door.' She had six or seven small children, all barefoot, all dirty. One grabbed the mother and said, 'Take him in there and show him where the 'possums and the 'coons come in at night.' There was a hole in the middle of the kitchen floor where animals came in, terrifying the children."

It had been easy to go after hearing that. So five months later, with only minor carpentry

"Ours is a beautiful county . . . we're at a high elevation, with glades something like your cranberry bogs. There's clean air, about 10,000 people, and one highway running the county's length."

skills, I nervously left my large home by the sea and my normal life as wife, mother, writer, and tutor. I was going to *give*.

Now here I was in steep, stunning mountains—sometimes mist enshrouded, other times fat and fluffy, when each tree stood out in singular relief. And deep among them I found three Appalachian women—and many men and women after that—who would change my life forever.

*B*ob headed the truck south first to a little town where a white Victorian house was being painted for a woman born in Victorian days herself. A few blocks away, a new septic system was being installed for a family whose eight fatherless children had not had tub baths since the Christmas before.

We turned west then, driving deeper into the country, past the face of an abandoned mine, then by lumber yards stocked with timber. "It usually moves out as fast as it comes in, but business is so bad, they're making mine props," Bob said, pointing to the four-by-four inch hardwood posts used to shore up mine shafts.

Further west, a work site sat in green isolation on a mountainside. To reach it, we parked on a dirt road, crossed a "crik" on a rickety footbridge, went through a cornfield then over a railroad track to finally scale a clay cliff. Easy for us: not easy for the invalid grandmother who lived inside the house.

We turned north then, up one mountain, down another. Groundhogs sat on their haunches by the roadside. "Some folks think they make good eating," Bob said. "Clean animals . . . vegetarians that forage in roadbeds for tender shoots." Further on, a mountaineer, rifle slung over his shoulder, awaited one.

*A*t our last stop, "Raccoon Holler," I met Stella Kessler, the first of many unforgettable mountain women. She strode toward us across a pasture on tanned, sturdy legs, her pale blue eyes just matching a homemade cotton blouse and skirt. About fifty-five, with blond hair streaming down her back, she was still a striking beauty.

Grabbing my hands warmly, she said, "If it weren't for work camp, we'd have no home." The house she had shared with her husband Joshua, who could not see, speak, or hear, had burned down the winter before. Now rising in the field behind her was a newly framed house being built on the old foundation.

To reach it, we parked on a dirt road, crossed a "crik" on a rickety footbridge, went through a cornfield then over a railroad track to finally scale a clay cliff. Easy for us: not easy for the invalid grandmother who lived inside the house.

Joshua had been "absolutely lost" since the
fire, confused by the unfamiliar place into
which they'd had to move. He wanted to be
back on ground where he grew up, where he
could leave the house and stroll to the
garden.

Joshua had been "absolutely lost" since the fire, confused by the unfamiliar place into which they'd had to move. He wanted to be back on ground where he grew up, where he could leave the house and stroll to the garden, fetch coal from the shed, even amble to the creek and cross the bridge.

Stella's love for him was legend. She had married him long before, despite her family's objections. Joshua could see some then, earning his living carving wood; but blindness, "which came on sudden-like when our little Josh was four," had robbed him of that.

Stella walked to the work site every day, delighted with the crew. When someone lifted a board, she hoisted the other end. And one day, she prepared a meal for them all, hauling it up the road herself.

Stella was a giver of inward light, communicating with Joshua by the language of touch. To get her attention, he'd pound her palm gently with his fist then trace his message on her arm, her fingers tapping information in return. As their house progressed, she guided him through, drawing his hand over two-by-fours, over insulation, across doorways then up to reach the rafters. More and more excited as it neared completion, Joshua again seemed the boy who'd been born on this spot; and when the floors were done, he got down on his knees and felt them all.

One crew member, disappointed that Joshua couldn't see the house, soon sensed "he was proud of it, and appreciated it by touching . . . putting his skin up against it and smelling the wood . . . this solid thing that someone had built."

Sixty miles south at the county's other end, my husband, Don—a skilled carpenter by avocation who went to work camp with me that first year—faced an imposing situation. He had pictured himself working on a mountainside with trees, fields, and sky. "Instead," he said, "the house I pulled up to was an ugly, reconditioned store in the center of a dirty main street, a factory raining soot on one side, a barroom on the other, a railroad just across, and big trucks rumbling by. I had a teenaged crew I'd just met, didn't know what they could do, and a list three pages long of things wrong with the place."

Home to Dick Cool (a previously unemployed coal miner who had recently found

He had pictured himself working on a mountainside with trees, fields, and sky. "Instead," he said, "the house I pulled up to was an ugly, reconditioned store in the center of a dirty main street, a factory raining soot on one side, a barroom on the other, a railroad just across, and big trucks rumbling by."

work), his wife, Vernie, and their seven kids, it had no bathroom, no hot water, no insulation or screens. Upstairs, a dark, central chamber, filled with bureaus and beds, had clothesline strung for closets. An enclosed upper porch had cracks that let in summer's heat and the sometimes minus-thirty degrees of winter. Outside, the porch was supported by four cinder-block columns, but a car had crashed into one—its replacement a rough-cut four-by-four.

The house and yard were full of kids, chickens, pups, kittens, and piles of accumulated this-and-that. "This is a two-week job that's going to take two *months*!" Don thought.

But he soon saw he had a remarkable crew. They built eighteen feet of closets in the upper porch, added a back porch, and tore up the old concrete front porch to build a wooden one where Vernie's kids could play. One teenager insulated the attic in its fierce heat while others dug a long trench through coal "gob" and rocks so a bathroom water line could be installed. When one of Don's crew fell ill, I took her place and stayed for days.

We all loved the constant Vernie Cool. If she wasn't checking on her kids, she was serv-

The house and yard were full of kids, chickens, pups, kittens, and piles of accumulated this-and-that. "This is a two-week job that's going to take two *months*!"

ing Kool-Aid to the crew. When I smelled something cooking on her stove one day, I called to ask her what it was. "White beans," she called back. They'd had brown beans the night before.

Vernie never left the house and never stopped working—washing, ironing, sweeping, mopping. I saw her asleep in the living room once, the washing machine rattling near her small, metal bed.

Sometimes we rested on the wooden front porch, the Cools' kittens cavorting on our outstretched legs; and the day we completed all our tasks, we gathered there to say a prayer. I surveyed the porch built, as my husband said, "of lumber so green it spit at you where the nails went in." I remembered pledges "to do our best" affixed to a cross the first day of camp. Then I noticed one of the kittens had climbed into a turned-down paper bag, curled up, and gone to sleep on a bed of nails.

Work campers paid room and board to live with county folk. Thus at an ensuing camp, I met strong, shy Lula McCoy when I stayed at her house. Lula was tiny and had the watchful eyes of the earth-mother she was. When we walked her spread at 3,000 feet, she showed me chickens, horses, kittens, dogs, and turkeys they'd raised from eggs. Would they later eat them? I asked. Oh no, she replied, they couldn't do that. Each had its own name and personality. Life was held dear, and it seemed apropos that even the cow emerging from the barn was pregnant.

Lula's handsome, silver-haired husband, Samuel, looked very much the mountain man astride his steady horse. This rugged coal miner told me in a warm, gravelly voice how he'd left his mountains for Ohio once but soon hurried back. He'd missed them too much.

Sitting barefoot on the porch one night, eating large, wild strawberries Samuel had picked, Lula spoke of the vision she'd had as a bride: a little girl standing at the foot of her bed, "all shimmering, shining white." She'd known then that she was pregnant, eventually bearing seven daughters and a son.

How they valued those children! They talked together of simple things each morning as Lula cooked their meal. And when a storm sprang up one evening, from my little room tucked under the eaves I heard them again conversing below. Vigilant Lula had gone into the yard and brought her sleeping brood in.

I loved it there: washing my hair with water from the rain barrel; trotting on a horse one evening after work; eating cooled cucumber slices floating in vinegar; overlooking her land with Lula at nightfall, listening to choruses of crickets and frogs.

Simplify, it all seemed to say. And *listen* to the rhythms of the earth, the home, and the heart.

She told me later of another storm. Its lightning had struck the house right by her sleeping son's head but left him untouched.

I loved it there: washing my hair with water from the rain barrel; trotting on a horse one evening after work; eating cooled cucumber slices floating in vinegar; overlooking her land with Lula at nightfall, listening to choruses of crickets and frogs.

Lula read a lot, and thought even more, and when she was troubled, she went into her woods. One day, deeply depressed, she'd entered the forest "praying to God to send a bear. A big, black bear." Instead, she said, he'd sent a deer—a great, large deer coursing over part of the property where there hadn't been a deer in years. Her husband and son ran for their guns. "Don't you shoot that ole deer! Don't you shoot that ole deer!" she'd cried.

She knew from whom it had come.

At quarter to six one morning, I left Lula's place to begin the long journey home. The sun was not yet up, the sky pellucid blue, the mist-filled pastures so dotted with daisies the horses seemed to be grazing in lace.

Simplify, it all seemed to say. And *listen* to the rhythms of the earth, the home, and the heart.

What did I know really? Only how to mix
mortar, hammer, and dig. And mine was to
be a complicated job, repairing a house 2,300
feet up on Tiller Mountain for a woman
named Hallie Hamrick.

3

Hallie's House

Now there are varieties of gifts, but the same Spirit.
1 CORINTHIANS 12:4

I'd never felt less like an adventuress. Bone weary, sleepless for twenty-six hours, I sat on the edge of a bed in the Pennsylvania home of people I'd only met the night before and looked across at the now-stirring Betty Ramsdell in the bed next to mine. How I'd envied her restful sleep during the night and the peaceful face dawn had revealed! I'd lain taut as a corkscrew, unable to relax from the tension of travel and the incessant, all-night chiming of a grandfather clock outside our bedroom door.

Betty—a former teacher and now young mother—and I were two of the drivers for a forty-two-member group from Massachusetts, heading for another West Virginia work camp. This Pennsylvania town was halfway, and by prearrangement with a church, we'd been housed overnight by its generous parishioners.

For weeks now I'd been anxiously awaking at 5 A.M. I'd attended work camp the summer before, but then I'd helped my husband, who

"Hi, Hallie," I said as we warmly shook hands.
"We've come to give you some help."

was skilled at carpentry. This time he couldn't go, and I was to have my own crew. What did I know really? Only how to mix mortar, hammer, and dig. And mine was to be a complicated job, repairing a house 2,300 feet up on Tiller Mountain for a woman named Hallie Hamrick.

While Betty dressed, I made notes in my journal. Then, too tired to care how I looked, I tucked my hair under a scarf, got dressed, and went to join our hosts. Ahead lay another day's drive into gradually ascending mountains—and for me it was leading to a mountaintop experience.

*L*ate in the afternoon, we finally arrived at our destination: the county's high school, elevation 2500 feet. We would gather here most evenings for sing-a-longs, a square dance, and discussion groups. After Bob Bondurant and Father Ken welcomed the two hundred work campers from various states, we ate dinner, got housing and crew assignments, then left for places we would call home for the next two weeks.

A mile down the county's main road lay Bill and Ginnie White's large farm, where a friend named Faith and I would stay. My husband and I had lived there the previous June, and I playfully told Faith we had the best accommodations at camp. Bill, county born and bred, was a fund of local lore. And I called Ginnie "the world's best cook," remembering her succulent meals of chicken and beef they had raised themselves and vegetables fresh from their garden.

I turned from the highway onto a long, uneven drive—a field of wildflowers on our right and directly ahead, on rising mountain pastures behind their home, the cows peacefully agraze.

How good it would be to see them again!

"I've decided I'm having the in-depth experience," Betty Ramsdell said the next morning as she joined crew leaders assembled in the high school auditorium to get work sites from Father Ken. "We had bears around and guns going off through the night!" She was staying in a town several mountains north of the school in a house with cold running water, an outhouse, and no shower or tub.

We sat in a circle introducing ourselves. Then Father Ken, who'd spent the spring approving and supplying sites, dispensed advice. He stressed safety, for there had never been a

Nearly fifty, she lived alone except for a six-year-old grandson, David, whom she was raising to lighten an ailing daughter's load.

serious accident at camp. "We just believe in God's presence, and in his protection, too."

I gathered my crew, all college students, eighteen or nineteen years old. From my Massachusetts town came two I barely knew: Mark, my crew coleader, and a tall brunette named Susie. The other two were strangers: another Sue—a small, blond work camp veteran from Florida—and a tall Pennsylvanian named Wes.

What will they be like? I wondered. We followed the county road north through the county seat then over the crest of Tiller Mountain to begin counting dirt roads. Hallie's would be the fourth on the right, a steep driveway, slanting up.

As we pulled in, Hallie emerged from the house: delicate, small boned, dark hair falling over her shoulders. Nearly fifty, she lived alone except for a six-year-old grandson, David, whom she was raising to lighten an ailing daughter's load.

"Hi, Hallie," I said as we warmly shook hands. "We've come to give you some help."

Mark and I surveyed the problems: windows, roof, and foundation sill to replace; front porch to enclose; house to insulate and paint. Mountain erosion had also taken a toll:

the sagging left side of the house was supported by too few log uprights, tilting fifteen degrees toward a steep, treed cliff. In the front yard were tires, an old washing machine, and various stacks of wood, which Hallie burned in her only heat source, a pot-bellied, living room stove.

We dug a trench to drain surface water from the sill and stacked wood in one neat pile, little David helping, too. In order to install cement-block supports, the boys spent time jacking up the house while the girls and I scraped the house, preparing it for paint. By day's end, delighted with my crew, I had nicknames for them all: Magnificent Mark, Wonderful Wes, Sensible Susie, and from Florida, Sweet-Sue.

Neater Nancy, Mark called me.

*I*n the days that followed, we saw that Hallie and David were unusually close, deeply secure in their love. The previous winter, Hallie had been sick; and David, then five, had made all her meals and stoked the stove with coal and wood.

The crew and I were also drawing together as we toiled at hard, dirty work that had its hazards. When we tore up the flooring of the rotten side porch, we found under the boards seven curled snakes. We pushed them aside to wriggle away.

During one especially trying day, Wes just missed being hit when a jack flew out as two cinder blocks broke. He also jumped off a slipping ladder just before it crashed to the ground. He fell through the side porch. Twice, he nearly ran a nail through his foot. And he was hit on the leg when Mark pulled up a board. "This," Wes said, "was a *dangerous* day!"

Mark had one eventful day, too. Climbing on an old bureau in Hallie's upstairs hall, he had hoisted himself into a dusty, ten-inch space between the roof peak and the ceiling in order to insulate. Nose and mouth covered, finding it hard to move and breathe, he inched forward, disappearing except for his feet. Sweet-Sue and I pushed insulation to him with a long, round stick. He got stuck crawling out (and later told us how scared he had felt) yet he was willing to squeeze into the hall's opposite space only to find a huge bees' nest and two live rats. He managed to insulate that side part of the way.

Before insulating eaves by David's room, we first had to spray for bees. "I killed rats in there once, too," said David. "Stepped on 'em with my foot." The fiberglass caused itchy arms and gagging throats, but when we were done, the eaves looked great.

As we sat singing at the high school that night, a crew leader who had stopped at Hallie's that day said, "I thought my site was complicated until I saw yours. You're doing a marvelous job!"

I was pleased with how well we worked together. What one member of my crew didn't know, another did. Wes could estimate distances ("that's one thing my father taught me," he said). Mark figured out how window glass was held in by pressure points then covered with glazing compound. Sweet-Sue could fill the staple gun. And Susie was artistic, painting Hallie's wash table and a handsome chair to match.

Driving to work each morning, we passed a large white sign with big black letters: God Makes House Calls. "That's us," I said to the crew. "Making a house call for God!"

In everything we did, Hallie worked with us, her common sense and self-sufficiency without end. When we needed a ladder, we used a hickory one she had built herself; when we needed a measure, she brought us a broom with a rule etched along its full length; and when we rolled out insulation, she suggested pressing it down with a smooth, flat stick to make the jackknife cut easier.

The winter before, she had scrambled onto her icy, leaking roof to secure tar paper with huge, heavy stones. Then she had covered her windows with thin, plastic sheets, nailing them firm with cardboard strips.

She got her water down by the drive in a sun-dappled, Eden-like glen. It trickled out from a pure mountain spring into a rubber pipe Hallie had rigged, the better to fill buckets for hauling to the house. Her spirit was indomitable, my respect ever deepening.

There was a dignity to everything Hallie did, whether working or laughing or sharing her life. With only six grades of schooling, she had wanted to complete her studies; but divorcing her husband years before, she had raised three children alone. Now she cared for David on a small welfare check supplemented by washing she did on her porch. Coal for their stove they collected by the road; the tires in the yard they collected to sell. Hallie had no running water, no bathroom, no radio or TV—and no self-pity in her sweet, sturdy soul.

In everything we did, Hallie worked with us, her common sense and self-sufficiency without end. When we needed a ladder, we used a hickory one she had built herself.

One morning, Hallie drew me aside, saying she had to leave for the day. "I don't have much, but I want you all to have something." She handed me five envelopes, an old penny in each. Written across each envelope were the words, *This is a token of love.*

On the Saturday between work weeks, Faith and I awoke to headaches, cloudbursts, and work camp's traditional day for a trip to a state park—one hour and three mountains away.

I felt anxious driving over, dreading a rainstorm on the mountain curves. But the skies kept their scudding clouds, and the young people sang all the way. When a deer darted across the road then turned on a hillside to watch us pass, I felt the linking of all living things.

Later, the skies broke to a glorious sun, and we swam, picnicked, laughed, and played, restoring ourselves for the week ahead. Sensible Susie had been aptly named; dependable always, she drove back through the mountains that night.

In the mornings, when I looked out my bedroom windows across the pastures of Bill White's farm, across the county road to see the yellow house where Susie was staying, I was warmed by the knowledge she was there. I realized how much the responsibility of work camp was shared. I needed Wes's height, Mark's expertise, Sweet-Sue's abilities, and Susie's driving skill when I was tired.

And they needed me to say, "OK, kids, let's do this, then this, then that!"

On Sunday I wrote in my journal:

If I had to distill this experience into a word, it would be 'honesty.' There's something about the simplicity of life here, and the wild, wonderfulness of the mountains that brings out what's basic in us. I haven't read a newspaper or watched TV in a week—my mind centered on the single thought: Hallie's house.

That day, as several of us waited in the county seat to greet newcomers arriving for the second week of camp, a young woman from my hometown and I walked partway through town, arms around each other's waists. "You know," she said, "kids I've known here a week, I feel I know better than kids I've known at home for years."

I knew what she meant. I never got into my car without a work camper discussing what was real in life: problems at school, conflicts at home, sex, commitment, marriage. One day, while having lunch on Hallie's porch, Wes shared how lonely he had felt as a high school student, and Susie told of her adoption as a child and how close she felt to her folks. In my adult evening study group, we discussed the nature of humankind; and Faith and I, late at night sprawled across my bed, comparing daily notes.

*M*ore aware of the dangers as we started the second week, I warned the crew to look around before lifting boards and—because Mark had already stepped on one—*to watch out for nails*! Persistent rains combined with Hallie's clay soil had also made a muddy morass. The footing treacherous, we held on with every step we took outside the house; and when we backed the car down the forty-five degree drive, brakes depressed to the floor, we sometimes slid all the way. Because Hallie's driveway began right around a mountain curve, one of us always stopped traffic until we had exited safely.

Monday afternoon, we added four to our

crew, and what welcome additions they were: a mother of five, a middle-aged man, and from Betty Ramsdell's crew my fifteen-year-old son. From Massachusetts, too, came teenaged Jennifer, a young woman I nicknamed "Mountain Goat." Unafraid of heights, she climbed surefootedly up a ladder onto Hallie's front porch roof then up onto an overturned barrel to help tar paper the upper roof—and not a moment too soon, for every time it rained, Hallie had to run up and down stairs, emptying pans kept under the eaves.

Father Ken arrived with supplies, taking our trash away in his truck; and Wanda, a neighbor of Hallie's, came by, looking—too late—for work camp help. Wanda was stout,

In the mornings, when I looked out my bedroom windows across the pastures to see the yellow house where Susie was staying, I was warmed by the knowledge she was there.

Little David had become an integral part of our crew. He could do so many things, and all well. Precocious, he prized his books and made people wash their hands before touching them.

assertive, and talked fast, offering beans and biscuits to anyone who would work for her.

A county electrician and work camp volunteer also stopped in. Horrified to find Hallie's lights all hooked to one line, he started to rewire. Then when I climbed out an upstairs window onto the back porch roof and noticed the frayed wires of the main electric line, I called him up to take a look.

"I'll have to send the power company to fix *that!*" he exclaimed.

Little David had become an integral part of our crew. He could do so many things, and all well. Precocious, he prized his books and

made people wash their hands before touching them. I noticed whenever I wrote in my journal, he snuggled close, watching me.

He knew every instant where each tool was, running to fetch what we needed. Our mother of five taught him to paint, and as I put a coat of paint on the house's back door,

I let him complete the last half. Hallie was watching. So was the smiling Wes as he ripped up flooring on the rotten back porch. He shook his head disbelievingly. "That kid isn't *human*," he said.

Hallie told us that David's faith was deeper than hers. As she'd driven home from town

Wednesday, too, saw the pieces falling into place. If we worked full tilt and had lots of help, we just might complete this assignment.

I had noticed how often during the two weeks helping hands were there when needed. When one of us sawed a board, another automatically held it.

the winter before, frightened by snow and slippery roads, she hadn't wanted to go on. "Don't worry, Grandmaw, if God had wanted us to went back, he'd a *told* us!" David said. She continued on, and though they saw other cars down in ditches, they made it safely home.

*T*he crew was showing exhaustion now, for a "bug" was sweeping through camp: fever, chills, intestinal complaints. Sweet-Sue slept in the car one whole day, and Mark stayed home another. How I missed his sensitive spirit and infectious *joie de vivre*! The first time we picked up Jennifer on the way in to work, we rounded a curve on a road new to us and saw a magnificent sight: an endless sea of mountains, valleys filled with clouds. As I stopped to photograph it, the impish Mark said, "I'm saving *my* film for a really *good* picture."

"Like when you're face to face with *God*?" I laughed.

*T*ears were trickling down Hallie's cheeks when we got to work on Wednesday. Wanda kept calling, pressuring Hallie, asking when a crew was coming to her house. "Am I taking you from others who really *need* you?" she asked.

Oh, Hallie, who needs it more? I thought.

I worried about Hallie's diet. She limped sometimes when her back and legs were ailing, and she also had arthritic hands. One day as she was stirring a pot of beans, she told me they would eat them for days. But for us that day, she lovingly, wordlessly laid out lemonade, a block of cheese, and a large box of fresh crackers. How much of her meager income had that taken?

Wednesday, too, saw the pieces falling into place. If we worked full tilt and had lots of help, we just might complete this assignment. Betty Ramsdell had promised us her last two days, along with the remainder of her crew.

"I'm beginning to get a little homesick," Susie said. "I called my parents last night, and when my father said, 'I love you,' my eyes filled with tears."

*A*t 2 A.M. Thursday, I sat bolt upright in bed, suddenly awake, my heart pounding. The curtains were blowing horizontally into the room on a queer, whistling wind. Thunder was crashing, the rain relentlessly drumming on the Whites' tin roof. As I had come up to bed, I had heard on their TV the tag end of a tornado warning.

Was this it?

I heard Ginnie White hurry upstairs, close windows in the hall, and check her visiting granddaughters, asleep in the room across from mine. Comforted, I snuggled back into my patchwork cocoon.

The heck with it!

We awoke to sun and a brilliant, blue-sky day, perfect for our work. Besides roofing, we started enclosing the front porch so Hallie would be warmer when she washed there in winter, and we welcomed a storm-window crew from county welfare who would install plexiglass windows throughout the house.

As Hallie and I drove to a store where she'd seen hammers on special sale, I spoke to her honestly. "You're so beautiful," I said. "You must have had chances to remarry."

"Oh, I had several," she replied, "but I thought they might not be kind to my children."

*T*hat night, at our last discussion group, we evaluated camp and talked of our crews. I pondered what had made mine so good.

Shared knowledge, first of all. What one knew, one taught; and no one knew it all. The

We gave Hallie a plant we'd bought and hung it from a wooden peg on the front of the house. Then, standing in a circle, hands joined, we conducted our last devotions on the new side porch. Hallie, crying softly, was the last to speak. "Sweet Jesus, protect them all as they go home, for I love ever' one of them."

jittery, pretrip woman I'd been had learned to tell the differences among various nails, to roof and insulate, and to build a porch.

Shared traditions, next. How we'd laughed over the car I drove. Loaned by a hometown man I called Mr G., it was a deluxe station wagon, air-conditioned, with C.B. and cruise control. We tried to treat it with tender care, but every time we loaded it with lumber, filled it with the crew, or bounced over yet another bumpy road, we chorused, "Poor Mr. G.!"

We had bonded, too, through daily devotions—those few minutes of prayer by woodpile, car, or porch. Another bond was the adventure itself. Strangers when we began, we were now a merry band. Early on, I'd asked the crew what the elements of our adventure were. The list had grown daily: discomfort, fear, courage, trust, surprise, laughter, fatigue.

But most of all, love.

After the meeting, I was driving some work campers to the home where they were staying. Turning off the county road, I crossed over a "crik" on a narrow wooden bridge, went over a railroad track—on the left a coal company, on the right loaded coal cars—then drove over a rutted road to where the young people got out in the family's drive.

During the day, a cow grazed in the family's pasture; but now it was empty, its grasses and the mountains beyond in black silhouette, overhung by a huge, yellow moon. I sat there in silence, totally tranquil.

"Thank you, God," I whispered, "for *everything*."

"Grandmaw, caint they stay another two weeks?" David asked Hallie on our last day there.

When we began the job, we had new, supple work gloves. Now we arrived each day to find them where Hallie had hung them above the porch—stiff, muddy soldiers marching on a beam. We had many hands to fill them that day as campers drifted in from already completed sites.

I had noticed how often during the two weeks helping hands were there when needed. When one of us sawed a board, another automatically held it; when we climbed ladders, others stationed themselves below; and when we leaned out windows, someone held us firm.

We were supposed to quit at noon and go to our houses to pack, but we worked steadily until four—except for Wes, who got picked up early. Although friendly, Wes wasn't demonstrative; but now he enfolded me in his arms and held me tight.

"Goodbye, Wes. God bless you."

Betty Ramsdell put the final flashing on Hallie's foundation while another camper disappeared into the outhouse to paint a big heart with leftover paint. And then, just as we finished the last bit of roofing, Sweet-Sue made a discovery. Lifting off an old portion of tar paper, she found a white, parchment-thin, discarded snakeskin.

In much the same way, Hallie's house had shed its old skin. Roofed, insulated, and wired, it had new porches front and side and six sturdy foundation supports to stop its down-mountain slide. With its foundation flashed and new windows installed, the house gleamed with two coats of paint.

But we, too, had taken on new colorations. Appalachia wouldn't be just a word to us now; it would always mean "Hallie." By leaving our homes and converging here, we had "lost our lives" for just a little while and found richer, more meaningful ones.

We gave Hallie a plant we'd bought and hung it from a wooden peg on the front of the house. Then, standing in a circle, hands joined, we conducted our last devotions on the new side porch. Hallie, crying softly, was the last to speak. "Sweet Jesus, protect them all as they go home, for I love ever' one of them."

We backed down the drive for the last time then, Hallie and David in front of the house, waving, the plant swinging gaily behind them.

I was destined to visit Hallie's house again. We corresponded after camp, my letters typed on heavy bond, hers handwritten on lined notebook paper. She signed them all, "Your mountain sister, Hallie."

Self-reliant though she was, I was concerned just the same. With a nearly spent pot-bellied stove, I thought about fire. That winter, I sent Hallie money from an article I'd sold; with tutoring money I bought a new stove; and after Christmas, I sent clothes bought on sale.

"I can never repay you," she said.

"Gift enough to know you," I replied.

At the next work camp, my site wasn't near her. But I was to spend my twenty-fifth wedding anniversary at that camp—without my husband, who was on a business trip a thousand miles away. And feeling lonely that

"I have something for you," she said. Her eyes were dancing, too, as she handed me a large package all wrapped in white. All my life—though I'd never mentioned it to anyone—I had wanted a quilt. Now here it was, given in this humble house, by my beautiful mountain friend.

night, I drove over three mountains to Hallie's house. I had missed her in the intervening year. As we threw our arms around each other, she danced a jig as she drew me into the house. "I have something for you," she said. Her eyes were dancing, too, as she handed me a large package all wrapped in white.

Inside was a multicolored, handmade quilt. All my life—though I'd never mentioned it to anyone—I had wanted a quilt. Now here it was, given in this humble house, by my beautiful mountain friend.

"I thought of you with every stitch," she said.

He was eleven when I gave him his first
driving lesson—so deep was my trust of his
instincts. That was the summer he looked
stricken when I left. "Shayne, if you love
someone, they're with you always. We're as
close as our thoughts," I said.

4
Shayne

I didn't even notice Shayne at first—this nine-year-old boy with black hair falling on his forehead, dressed in a too-small T-shirt. My work camp coleader and I were too busy figuring how best to underpin the modest trailer home Shayne shared with his mother, brother, and sister.

But then I noticed he was everywhere. When we needed another hammer, he knew where one was. And he could always find our tin snips, level, and tape when asked. If there was digging to be done, he was there with a shovel. If there was wood to be measured, he had a pencil in his hand. He was invaluable to us, just as he has been invaluable at each work camp since. Shayne eventually became a legitimate crew member, and he has painted, insulated, and repaired roofs of the aged, sick, and needy with adult aplomb and ability.

But his greatest gifts are character and grace.

We became fast friends that June when we met because work camp was transferred to his county. One day, as Shayne and I drove to the local store for more supplies, he pointed out grazing horses, lilies bending by the roadsides, the mist hanging in distant mountain valleys. "Ain't it beautiful here?" he asked. This eye for outer beauty was matched by his inner insights. "I ain't never going to drink beer nor take no drugs," he said. "I'm going to keep ma' mind *clear*!"

And Shayne shared what he had. When we gave him candy, he said he'd had some already. "I'll save this for my friend," he said. While he taught us generosity, I taught him to use my 35mm camera, listening to his delighted gasp as the telephoto lens brought close the shoulder-high rye grass in his backyard.

He was eleven when I gave him his first driving lesson—so deep was my trust of his instincts. That was the summer he looked stricken when I left. "Shayne, if you love someone, they're with you always. We're as close as our thoughts," I said.

The year he was twelve, his schoolwork slipped due to trouble with an uncaring teacher. But after the first semester, he righted himself. "If *I* don't care, I ain't gonna make it!" he said. The following year, along with his best friend Keith, he won the Social Studies Medal

He pointed out grazing horses, lilies bending by the roadsides, the mist hanging in distant mountain valleys. "Ain't it beautiful here?" he asked.

I noticed he was everywhere. When we needed another hammer, he knew where one was. And he could always find our tin snips, level, and tape when asked. If there was digging to be done, he was there with a shovel. If there was wood to be measured, he had a pencil in his hand. He was invaluable to us, just as he has been invaluable at each work camp since.

for the sixth-grade level in the state of West Virginia.

At age twelve, too, during work camp, he helped repair a ramshackle house in near 100-degree heat—without complaint. On our last day there, he suddenly announced, "Will all adults please gather round for a moment of appreciation? Me and Keith has went into the woods and picked these wild raspberries for you. We've taken a vow not to eat one of 'em ourselves." Knowing how much he savored the fruit made sweeter the gift in his upturned shirt.

"Are you rich?" Shayne asked me when he was thirteen, commenting on the kind of car I drove.

"I'm rich in friends, Shayne. People like you."

But if he was curious, he could be reassuring, too. As we reached the crest of Moses Mountain driving back from work, we saw some abandoned beagle pups running beside the road. "Don't worry," he calmly said. "They'll make their way to somebody's house, and they'll be taken in."

Shayne was fifteen at last summer's camp— all unlaced sneakers, long, mod hair, and growing tall to match the size of his large, skillful hands. He took time off from constructing a porch to take me to campers working at an isolated site.

In order to reach them, we parked on a dirt road and walked for a while, first passing houses with occupants sitting in the sun: an autistic savant who called sports scores to Shayne, a man with a sewn-shut eye and chewing tobacco staining his chin, and other worn-out souls the world would never note.

"Will all adults please gather round for a moment of appreciation? Me and Keith has went into the woods and picked these wild raspberries for you. We've taken a vow not to eat one of 'em ourselves."

In order to reach them, we parked on a dirt road and walked for a while, first passing houses with occupants sitting in the sun . . . "I come up here a lot," Shayne said. "These people are all my friends."

"I come up here a lot," Shayne said. "These people are all my friends."

Ralph Waldo Emerson said we love honor and pay it homage, no matter in whom it is shown. And Shayne had honor—even at nine. That first summer with him, there was a ves-

per service near work camp's end by a campfire deep in the woods. But when it was over, the path back was dark. Walking in front of me, Shayne suddenly reached around. "Here, take my hand," he said assuringly. "I'll show you the way."

His greatest gifts are
character and grace.

We passed other houses set deep in verdant shade, but the Adkins' house sat in a clearing, absorbing the searing sun.

5
The House Where Miracles Met

In my Father's house are many mansions.
JOHN 14:2 (KJV)

A week after we got home, I still had dirt under my fingernails, still had the remnants of a sore throat, and still felt exhausted. My car's muffler and air conditioner were broken, and there was a slow leak in the right rear tire. But I felt exhilarated, too, by an Appalachian encounter of the miraculous kind.

1987—my thirteenth work camp—and the old mystique had operated again. Years before, in Massachusetts, a friend had asked why I went back year after year. "Oh . . . the mountains . . . the people . . . the adventure. . . ." My voice had trailed off, for some experiences defy neat packaging. I simply knew I had to go.

And not just me.

Why did so many others return? "There's a list of twenty-two things to do on my desk at home," said a man from Miami. "But when I'm at work camp, I just forget everything else." For a young woman in her teens, it was "a chance for my insides to grow and another outlook for my mind to have." For a woman like my friend Faith—busy wife, mother,

Though work camp is a collective experience, it's also a singular one, bounded by each crew's special circumstances.

teacher, tennis coach—it was "the complete change, work, and relaxation rolled into one."

There was another side to it, too. "Don't forget you'll be coming not only to minister but to be ministered to," said a Baptist minister who had attended work camp since its inception. And he was right. Widows, widowers, and divorced people had found healing there. Some young people had found future mates. Everyone's life, in fact, was enriched and enlarged.

Perhaps a young man, describing where he stayed one year at camp, symbolically summed it up best: "When I got back to where I'm living, the night was so dark, and the fireflies so thick, it was like walking in stars."

That was it—like walking in stars. Only it wasn't stars Marcia Bansley and I saw as we headed north to camp on Atlanta's Interstate 75 that June day in 1987; it was buckets of rain. By the time we'd crossed the Kentucky border four hours later, however, the sky was bright with billowy clouds, perfect weather for the five-hour drive that still lay ahead.

For years I'd driven to camp from Massachusetts, but since 1982, when my husband's business had brought us south, I'd journeyed from the opposite direction. Marcia, executive director of an environmental nonprofit organization, was making her second trip. We'd met in Atlanta two years before, when I'd interviewed and photographed her for a magazine article I was preparing, and we had been good friends ever since.

The Reverend Bob Bondurant had also changed locale. In 1983, he had said good-bye to his rural church and undertaken a campus ministry in another part of West Virginia. He'd shifted camp—now shortened to a week—to a county an hour's drive south of his university.

This county's mountains may not have been as high as the other county's and the poverty may not have been as acute, but the needs were still great. Marcia and I, along with participants from nine states who'd come to help, were welcomed one Sunday to the work camp centered at the facilities of the county's state park.

Here in a mess hall we would dine twice a day. Young people would bunk in park barracks while most adults stayed in park cabins or with county folk nearby. Evening activities took place in the park's pavilion. Two miles away lay the Presbyterian Chapel where we'd pick up and return tools each day.

Bob Bondurant led Monday's orientation,

speaking of sensitivities required, curfews to be obeyed, and care needed using power tools. Then we spread throughout the county to work at thirty projects in all, from Little Branch to Sycamore Hollow, Fort Gray to Moses Fork.

Though work camp is a collective experience, it's also a singular one, bounded by each crew's special circumstances. Marcia's and my project required the camp's most extensive work: completing the basic shell of Gail and Philip Adkins' house in exactly four and a half days. The project had been located by Sister Roberta Feil, one of three Catholic nuns living and working in the county, who also volunteered at camp.

We began with ten crew members. Besides us Georgians, our crew included Ohio insurance salesman David Brunk and Sister Martha Werner, the Catholic campus chaplain at Seton Hall University in New Jersey. There were also six West Virginians—former Marine and retired service station supplier Ed Miller, nineteen-year-old carpenter Joe Racer, plus four county kids: Shayne and his brother Billy, Shayne's best friend Keith, and Keith's cousin Adrena—all twelve or thirteen years old.

The Adkins' house was an hour's drive from camp headquarters through summer's steamiest heat—over curving mountain roads, past coal tipples, coal trains, laden coal trucks spewing nauseous smoke, through the small town of Fort Gray, then onto a dusty road that twisted for several miles more. We passed other houses set deep in verdant shade, but the Adkins' house sat in a clearing, absorbing the searing sun.

As we pulled in, Mrs. Adkins, a forty-two-year-old woman buttered brown by weather and lined by adversity, appeared in the doorway. Barefoot, with red hair falling in two braids, she spoke with a husky twang. Her husband, Philip, was forty-six and alcoholic, tanned, unshaven, his head and eyes cast downward most of the time. A carpenter by trade, he had fallen on terrible times—car stolen, no work, and now a sudden "spell." Mrs. Adkins said he'd screamed that morning and fallen from bed, unconscious with a seizure. Their son, Wesley, twelve, was barefoot, barechested, and dirty head to foot. "I'm allergic to soap," he said.

The house was small, maybe twenty-six feet long by twenty feet wide, built from construction leftovers Mr. Adkins had found. There was a henhouse (in which they'd lived

As we pulled in, Mrs. Adkins, a forty-two-year-old woman buttered brown by weather and lined by adversity, appeared in the doorway. Barefoot, with red hair falling in two braids, she spoke with a husky twang.

In the kitchen stood an iron wood-burning stove, stoked even in the summer heat, warming pan bread and sauerkraut cooked some time before. An unhooked electric stove sat uselessly nearby.

while he built the house), storage shed, outhouse off to one side, and vegetable gardens front and back. Farther back, where the land sloped down, loaded coal trains regularly rumbled by.

Inside, the house was dark and dusty, each room crammed. A small living room held a sofa, table, chair, TV, and the Adkins' bed, which was by the pot-bellied stove. One light bulb hung there and another hung in the kitchen, both dangerously jury-rigged with the TV to a telephone pole in the yard. In the kitchen stood an iron wood-burning stove, stoked even in the summer heat, warming pan bread and sauerkraut cooked some time before. An unhooked electric stove sat uselessly nearby.

These two rooms had the only insulation and wallboard, obtained the winter before by Sister Roberta to stave off the cold. Behind them stood a partially wall-boarded bedroom, plus studding for a second bedroom and eventual bath. The hall was so dark that we didn't see curled-up Brutus, the family dog, and we stepped on him more than once. There was no running water, no plumbing, no place to hang clothes.

Glamor is shed quickly at camp. Our faces flushed, makeup ran, and clothes clung as we, along with the men, inventoried work: tin roof to repair, siding to be put on, spackling and sanding to be done on the installed wallboard, attic to insulate, insulation and wallboard to be put up in remaining rooms, house to be painted inside and the trim out. The house needed complete wiring as well, and two retired electricians had volunteered to work one day.

When Mrs. Adkins led me behind the house on the way to the "crik" to see their water supply, I noticed one exterior back panel missing, the exposed studding charred.

Someone had tried to burn them out the previous November, she said, "but we got to it in time." Mrs. Adkins held her legs stiff when she walked, swinging each in an arc from the hip. Her back was in constant pain, but the doctors had not determined why. Though the nuns saw that she received therapy, the pain had not eased.

The creek was down a slippery slope, thick with bushes and trees, and I wondered how she scrambled up and down—not that it mattered much right then. It was nearly dry except for a few mud puddles.

Mr. Adkins sat on the outside steps, sharpening tools, for he worked with us from the first day on. He had muscled arms and skillful hands, and I thought about how sad it was he drank. Sister Roberta said he had joined A.A. but wasn't doing well "so far."

There's something about rural life that makes kids competent, and the youngsters on our crew dug right in. They sanded the spackling or scurried up the ladder to mark leaks in the roof. The men began cutting a doorway through the back living room wall to give more ventilation while Sister Martha started what she would do all week. She blithely painted everything in sight—walls, doors, win-

Sister Martha started what she would do all week. She blithely painted everything in sight—walls, doors, windows, ceilings—turning darkness into light.

dows, ceilings—turning darkness into light.

We used the Adkins' outhouse when necessary, Adrena accompanying me to watch the path for privacy. The outhouse stood next to a raspberry patch; so before entering, I always checked for snakes. Driving back to camp headquarters after work, Adrena told us about a neighbor of hers for whom she baby-sat. Once, after the woman inadvertently left a screen door ajar, a copperhead had slid in, settling under the sofa cushions to lay its eggs. Later when the neighbor sat down, the snake slithered out, passing down by her legs.

After supper in the mess hall, served by county women as their participation in camp, Marcia and I went to Ben and Belle Lambert's where we were sleeping for the week. Known countywide, Belle worked in school administration. Ben was central to camp, identifying work sites then hauling materials to each.

It was wonderful to bathe at the Lamberts',

the bathroom clean and luxurious. And it was good to get cool again. *But what about the Adkins?* I thought. How would they wash up? In my journal that night, I made a single note: "Hotter today than I've ever felt."

To supply our site with water, from Tuesday on we filled plastic milk jugs at the Lamberts and crammed them into my car trunk. And it was good we did, for each day dawned as hot as the next—95 degrees, humidity to match.

There was a rhythm to our work: "Everyone a leader and follower according to talents and skills, and shifting as we went along," as Marcia later described it. When Marcia realized the electricians couldn't finish on the only day they said they could work, she learned from them how to wire the receptacles. And when they needed more supplies, it was Adrena who guided me into town. Only twelve, she seemed a peer, wise and adept beyond her years. Thanks to Sister Martha and her kids' brigade, whose paint-flecked faces resembled robin eggs, the house was becoming bright.

Mr. Adkins's face was brightening, too, losing its defeated look. A doctor had volunteered two days' free exams at the chapel, and David Brunk had driven Mr. Adkins in. In turn, Mr. Adkins helped us with his carpentry advice. Though he was very quiet, and mumbled when he spoke, he had an inner sweetness we all felt.

It was plain that he rarely left Mrs. Adkins's thoughts, her glances filled with respectful concern. Although he was sick, disheveled, and desperately needed dental care, she adored him. And that love extended to their son, Wesley. Sister Martha learned that after the fire, fearing for Wesley's welfare, Mrs. Adkins had risen at five o'clock each morning to walk him two miles to the school bus then two miles back, repeating the process each afternoon.

We were incredulous. On those legs? In that pain?

I've read that "a miracle really represents the sudden recognition of the good already at hand." So I came to call the Adkins' place "the house where miracles met." It wasn't just the young people, who, when they weren't sanding or painting, were squeezing into the furnacelike attic to insulate; nor retired Ed Miller, who toiled like a Trojan, never mentioning the medication he took or the daily naps he would normally have; nor young Joe Racer,

Ed Miller toiled like a Trojan, never mentioning the medication he took or the daily naps he would normally have.

who worked tirelessly installing wallboard. Nor was it the reinforcements that came in midweek: a tall, retired, aristocratic minister and his wisp of a wife from the university city, who worked as if they were twenty, and their daughter-in-law with her two children, learning to serve at ages nine and eleven.

It was also those people who appeared as special needs arose. Late our first afternoon, a friend of Mrs. Adkins's dropped by: Rosemary Marcum, 241 pounds, down from 303, on her way to 120 and still rash-covered from a bout with Rocky Mountain spotted fever. The next afternoon, after a crashing thunderstorm revealed a roof beyond repair, she suddenly reappeared with her husband. At thirty, Jeffrey Marcum was a professional roofer, currently unemployed. He suggested using the new house siding for the roof and said he'd do the work if we campers bought the plywood sheathing needed underneath.

The electricians, too, returned a second day. "We couldn't *not* come," they said, finishing work that would have cost two thousand dollars if the Adkins had had to pay. When Joe Racer needed to leave, an unemployed area lad unexpectedly motorcycled in, using his strength to shove heavy furniture so the young people could paint walls and his height to spackle spots near the ceiling. And a plumber friend of Mr. Adkins's, temporarily out of work, had the skills to run heavy-duty wire above the roof in galvanized pipe. Then he wired the outside meter box so the power company would come for the final hookup.

Another miracle was yet to come after Wesley and I talked seriously about soap.

"The power company's here!" Mrs. Adkins's voice announced triumphantly on Friday. Her excitement was palpable as the men dismantled and carried the iron stove to the yard then plugged in the electric one.

There's something about rural life that makes kids competent, and the youngsters on our crew dug right in.

A plumber friend of Mr. Adkins's had the
skills to run heavy-duty wire above the roof
in galvanized pipe. Then he wired the outside
meter box so the power company would
come for the final hookup.

There was a rhythm to our work: "Everyone a leader and follower according to talents and skills, and shifting as we went along."

The house bustled like a beehive, people finishing tasks, moving in and out. Another work camp crew arrived with a half-ton truck to haul away the trash while still another unemployed plumber friend of the Adkins' appeared, looking over the proceedings. It was ludicrous, I told him, that Mrs. Adkins had a sink piled with dishes she couldn't wash because there was no place for the water to drain out. When he said he'd fix a drain if he only had the parts, I had him write a list then took Shayne and Keith with me to the hardware store at Fort Gray.

With the temperature nearing 100 degrees, and no air-conditioning at the store—and still battling the sore throat I'd had all week—I felt faint as the older woman, the owner, slowly collected collars, clamps, and PVC pipes. Knowing it was for Mr. Adkins's house, she said, "He was a good carpenter once—before he drank."

"Oh, he's joined A.A.," I told her, and she smiled in obvious surprise.

What a sight we must have been as we

Hadn't we all been changed in a way? We had been a ragtag band of adventurers, imperfect every one, but each giving what we had. In working together at this impoverished house, we had seen beneath the surface Mr. Adkins's courage and Mrs. Adkins's unconditional love.

slowly drove back, swaying over the last dusty stretch of rutted road, ten-foot PVC pipes protruding from the car windows, encircled by young boys' arms!

Later, our work complete, it was time to leave. After hugs all around, we backed out of the yard—the Adkinses waving, Wesley smiling cheerfully, clean as could be from head to foot.

But our miracles were not through yet. Bothered by the Adkins' water situation, Marcia and I decided while driving home to have a well installed for them. Through donations we covered the costs.

After her summer vacation, Sister Roberta visited the Adkinses and couldn't believe the change. The house was neat inside, they had made two new closets, and the yard was completely cleaned up. The henhouse and shed had been freshly painted, and Mr. Adkins had constructed another shed from trees he had cut in the woods. The lady in the hardware store had offered him some carpentry work, and he was busy on other jobs. He had gotten an old car and some advice from his doctors. From late June on, he hadn't touched a drop of alcohol and was proud of his coins from Alcoholics Anonymous.

Late in November, a letter came from Mrs. Adkins, saying how much they liked the new well. Then she added, "It has been five months since Philip quit drinking, and I thank God every day. I can't explain how it's changed our lives."

But hadn't we all been changed in a way? We had been a ragtag band of adventurers, imperfect every one, but each giving what we had. In working together at this impoverished house, we had seen beneath the surface Mr. Adkins's courage and Mrs. Adkins's unconditional love.

And I knew we had all been blessed. Jesus said, "Just as you did it to one of the least of these who are members of my family, you did it to me" (Matt. 25:40). One day, in the Adkins' back bedroom, their tattered, tacked-back curtain caught my eye. The late afternoon sun illuminated the place where worn fibers had fallen out.

Its shape was a small, ragged cross.

One day, in the Adkins' back bedroom, their tattered, tacked-back curtain caught my eye. The late afternoon sun illuminated the place where worn fibers had fallen out.

Ben found the perfect wife in Belle, marrying
the cream of the county, when he was
twenty-two and she still a high-school senior
just turning eighteen.

6

The Enduring Duke and Duchess

Cast your bread upon the waters, for you will find it after many days.
ECCLESIASTES 11:1 (RSV)

I call Ben Lambert the Duke of his county for good reason. A big man in every way—tall, well built, character so formidable that tales are legion—this retired coal miner and former deputy sheriff is respected by everyone, even sons of men he sent to jail.

Ben found the perfect wife in Belle, marrying the cream of the county, when he was twenty-two and she still a high-school senior just turning eighteen. They skipped over to Kentucky to tie the knot then rode the bus back across the bridge that separates Kentucky from West Virginia. Belle went directly home, not informing her parents of the nuptials for two weeks. If they weren't completely devastated by her marriage to a young man raised on welfare, recently discharged from the service and jobless, they were certainly disappointed. They probably thought Ben wouldn't amount to a hill of beans.

But Ben and Belle prevailed, Ben eventually becoming the best-known man in the county

Ben spends the spring selecting work sites,
for his finger is still very much on the
county's pulse, just as his heart is deeply
involved in the community's religious life.

and Belle recently retiring after a distinguished forty-two-year career in teaching and school administration. If Ben is the county's Duke, she is surely its Duchess.

I stay with the Lamberts for a week each June after traveling from Atlanta to attend work camp. Ben spends the spring selecting work sites, for his finger is still very much on the county's pulse, just as his heart is deeply involved in the community's religious life. And his hands helped build the Presbyterian Chapel, the center of many work camp activities.

There's not an ounce of arrogance in this hard worker, who, by any measure, should have been dead from the same coronary artery disease that prematurely killed his father and two brothers. "I'm too ornery to die." He chuckles, dismissing his medical history, but I think he's still here because he's needed by so many.

Some Junes I don't work with a crew but rather travel the mountain roads with Ben in his truck, delivering supplies and photographing camp for audiovisual presentations. Trips with him are a writer-photographer's dream. Ben points out where he once shut down moonshine stills and tells, in his rich vernacular, how he used to corral wrongdoers. If he knew them, they'd be personally informed of the hour to arrive at jail; if he didn't know them, he would send a letter. No-shows would be pulled from bed at 2 A.M. by Ben himself and escorted to the pokey by the seat of their pants.

Ben's tenacity was shaped by a childhood that left scant time for play. His parents divorced when he was three, his father moving away, his mother raising five children alone. Their cold, too-small house lacked underpinning, insulation, and indoor plumbing. Chores reigned constant: cows to be milked on the small working farm, water to be drawn from the well, garden to be tended. And then there was studying to be done at the two-room schoolhouse he attended until high school.

This spartan rural life changed abruptly in 1942 when Ben was drafted at age seventeen and set sail across the Atlantic during World War II. As part of the Army's 34th Infantry Division, he saw action in Africa and Sicily then stormed ashore at Anzio Beachhead in Italy. There he was wounded by flying shrapnel and hospitalized, unable to walk for weeks.

Starting as a private, Ben had risen quickly through the ranks: corporal, sergeant, staff sergeant, making master sergeant by the time he saw the executed dictator Mussolini hanging by his heels in the square in Milan. War's end found him on the Austrian border, capturing a Russian captain who had first been seized by the Germans and made to fight Americans.

Ben had seen enough of death and, once back home in the county, he immediately chose life. In the single most important decision he would ever make, he reached for quality, meeting and marrying the beautiful Belle McEwan in a breathtaking two weeks.

He first found work in the coal mines, and fourteen months later their daughter Jennie-Sue arrived. "She was born in a company house, delivered by a company doctor, and paid for by payroll deduction," he says. Ben now had a wife, a job, and a child. It was time to find his father.

For twenty years, Ben had neither seen nor heard from his dad. But one Sunday afternoon, after learning his father was living in a certain Virginia town, Ben—accompanied by Belle, one of his sisters and her husband— drove the three-hour distance. Nearing their destination, they passed an old car going in the opposite direction. Ben suddenly shouted,

"Stop! That's my father!" They turned around, chased the car down, and, said Ben, "it *was* my father."

Their meeting was easy. "He embraced me, took us to his house, fed us, and introduced me to two half-sisters I didn't know I had." And their relationship remained loving. "He was a sickly man, and I later went back, got him, and took him before a board of doctors." Ben and his dad visited each other often until the end of his father's life. For that which was lost had been found.

Coal miners didn't make much money in those days, and after four years, Ben found work in the automobile industry—first in Cleveland, Ohio, and then on a Detroit assembly line, coming home once or twice a month to Belle and Jennie-Sue. Five years later— his family's size now increased by a second daughter, Barbara Jean—Ben returned to the county for good.

For a time, he drove a commercial bus, leaving that to become simultaneously a school bus driver and the county's deputy sheriff. On the first day of school each year, Ben stood in front of the bus, outlining to the high schoolers his set of rules: "No arms out the windows, no water guns, no flippin' with

rubber bands, no smokin', and no alcohol." And if they broke the rules, they'd be off the bus for good.

So persuasive was his presence, no one got kicked off.

Wily and with-it, authoritative and unafraid, Ben was an excellent lawman. As we traversed Blue Moon Holler one day, I asked how many moonshine stills he had shut down. "Oh, mercy, plenty!" He laughed. Stopping his truck, he pointed up a tangential dirt road. "I arrested a feller at the head of that holler once, makin' whiskey in a gas meter house. He was boiling mash with fire from the gas line so there wouldn't be any smoke."

I asked him how he knew that.

Chores reigned constant: cows to be milked on the small working farm, water to be drawn from the well, garden to be tended.

Smiling quizzically, he said, "Why, honey, I could *smell* it!"

Among other duties, Ben broke up brawls at beer joints and investigated breakings and enterings. One day, after spotting three men passing stolen goods out a store window then into their car, he waited up the road where they would have to pass. He stopped the vehicle, only to be met by a gun when the driver rolled down the window. His reflexes quick, Ben seized the man's arm. The gun discharged through the roof.

Murder cases fascinated him most. "Many perpetrators tried to deny their guilt, and some attempted bribes," he told me. "Oh, I've been offered lots of money to turn my head before their cases came up, *but I would not take it*! I swore an oath, and I wasn't sending my soul to hell for a bunch of criminals."

Ben ended his working life where it began— in the mines. During his twenty-year stint, "I did it all—" he says, "laid track, set timbers, operated a cutting machine that cut coal before it was dynamited, loaded coal into a shuttle car with a loading machine that took it to a conveyor belt, and ran a motor that brought the coal outside."

The last mine in which Ben worked tunneled four miles through three mountains, maintaining a constant 65 degrees summer and winter, with two airways, one incoming, the other outgoing. He would walk in 300 feet, then crawl aboard a car powered by a 300-volt overhead wire to ride the rest of the way. Along with other miners, he worked for eight hours in a forty-inch-high space without once coming into the fresh air—and always supplied with an emergency gas mask.

He loved it all as he has loved his life. "I feel blessed," he says. And then he adds, "If I've done anybody wrong, I shore don't know it!"

*B*elle McEwan Lambert was a modern woman long before the days of feminism. But then, she was born of a trendsetting woman. Decades before women routinely combined family life with careers, Belle's mother, Lily McEwan, bore twelve children and raised nine to adulthood while teaching school for thirty-five years. Belle was the baby of the family and learned Lily's lessons well.

Lily Bowens was a tall, intelligent, dark-haired beauty when, at twenty-one, she married twenty-four-year-old Roderick McEwan. At sixteen, she had taken and passed the state teacher's examination in all phases of cur-

Ben ended his working life where it began—in the mines. During his twenty-year stint, "I did it all—" he says.

riculum. That allowed her to skip the rest of high school, and she began to teach in elementary school while earning a college associate degree. Lily lived elsewhere in West Virginia then; but following their marriage, Rod brought her to the county, where they bought property and built a house. She resumed teaching, and Rod left the timber business, becoming a storekeeper.

Belle's childhood was idyllic in a county she describes as a place of peace and plenty. "The mountains weren't treed down to the creeks in those days like they are now," she says. "The 'bottoms' or flatlands were all farms and hay. *Everybody* farmed, and our farm had horses, cows, chickens, sheep, ducks. Dad had hay wagons, and we had a huge orchard—apple trees that flowered in spring and three rows of peach trees. All the yards had flowers, and homes were neatly kept . . . all elements were there for peaceful living."

There was no welfare; everyone in the community worked. "I can't remember peo-

The Lamberts live in the house where Ben grew up although it has long since been enlarged and modernized. Ben tends two expansive vegetable gardens on their large acreage, sharing the bounty with neighbors.

ple being impoverished like they are now. Two families were really poor and everyone helped them, but they had pride and also helped themselves. People were engaged with their families and the land."

Belle's dad provided the earthy, abundant setting, and her mother gave it soul. "We had an organ, and all the children gathered around as she sang to us, and we to her." Lily also strengthened their resolve. "You go to school, you succeed, you make something of your lives," she urged.

Belle needed no scholastic prompting; hers was a mind of crystal clarity, which she kept constantly filled. "I wouldn't have skipped a day of school for anything. I was scared to death I might miss something! I wanted to be involved, and I was—in everything. I *wanted* to achieve; all the kids I grew up with wanted to go to school and wanted to be somebody."

Then she met Ben.

How he must have captured her imagination! Until then, she'd only dated boys in her class, "but Ben was so different." This was a man who had *been* places, *done* things, was an *adventurer!* And how she must have captivated him with fine features inherited from her mother and with the fair complexion, strawberry-blond hair, and pale blue eyes of her father.

Spontaneous as Belle's decision was to marry Ben, it didn't deter her from her goal: education. Married in January, she was graduated from high school in May, and in September—three months pregnant—she started classes at the university, an hour's drive north. "I never gave up a class," she says, even after Jennie-Sue was born.

Two years later, barely twenty, Belle got a job as secretary in a high school, working full time during the day, carrying thirteen credit hours of university studies in the evening.

Upon completing two years of college, she got a "Standard Normal" teaching certificate—the equivalent of sixty-four credit hours—and, at twenty-one, she started teaching. It was a one-room schoolhouse way up a path on a mountain road, but it was her *world.*

She remained there more than two years. Ben sometimes drove her to work through deep winter snows. When their car and the school bus couldn't make it all the way, Belle would lead her little charges up the final steep path, a pied piper of learning. Evenings found her back at the university, finishing her undergraduate degree.

Teaching at another school followed—one fourth-grade class, then two fifth grades. But when a new school opened, Belle was transferred there, where she would teach first grade for seventeen years. She loved the children who fell under her wing—and they her—but one class so won her heart that she asked to move along with them to second grade.

Her observations acute, Belle once told Ben that after working for six weeks with first-graders, she could determine who would later be successful, which ones would "get by," and the few who would have great struggles in life. "Most of the time it went back to the home environment," she says. "Some came to first grade and had never had a book in their hands."

Before long Belle's excellence was recognized, and she won scholarships to a university to work two summers on a specialization in reading disabilities. Ben was working out of state, and Lily took care of the two daughters to whom Belle would always remain close. When the National Teacher Corps came along, she was tapped to be a lead teacher, spending three years in the government program. Along with the position came an increase in salary and the chance to work on her master's degree at government expense.

She became a school principal, eventually moving into school administration, beginning as supervisor of county classroom teachers. She attended conferences at Notre Dame, West Virginia University, and elsewhere while also completing enough hours for a doctorate—which she didn't obtain formally, feeling it no longer necessary. At retirement, Belle was director of the county's elementary education program—in charge of all curriculum, running principals' meetings, and purchasing all textbooks.

A natural aristocrat, Belle's taste is as impeccable as her first-rate mind: in books, clothes, jewelry, and in the blue Mercedes she purchased when retirement was imminent. "It wasn't a status symbol," she says. "I simply wanted quality."

Quality is what her life has been about. She has taught generations of students, mentoring their teachers along the way. Ask what has been her greatest joy, and her eyes soften. She smiles her slow, sweet smile and replies, "Children. Working with children."

"God has been good to me," says Belle Lambert—a woman who wears silk pajamas beneath which beats a golden heart.

*T*he Lamberts live in the house where Ben grew up although it has long since been enlarged and modernized. Ben tends two expansive vegetable gardens on their large acreage, sharing the bounty with neighbors. Belle has planted the house's commodious yard, fenced to enclose their two pets: an enthusiastic golden retriever named Daniel and Miss Fifi, a sleek, gray cat.

Colorful flowers grace the property: daylilies, roses, zinnias, and pink impatiens. The impatiens ring the base of a stately maple that was given as a seedling tree to Belle many

Colorful flowers grace the property: daylilies, roses, zinnias, and pink impatiens. The impatiens ring the base of a stately maple that was given as a seedling tree to Belle many years ago by a class in her one-room school.

years ago by a class in her one-room school. A birdhouse hangs from one branch, and bird feeders perch near the neighboring apple tree.

Ben built a long side porch onto the house with columns supporting the roof, where birds nest under the eaves. At eventide, Belle glories in sitting on the porch, watching dusk descend as mist rolls down the mountains. "I love the quietness and peace," she says. The porch also plays host to a multitude of visitors: their daughters and sons-in-law, three beloved grandchildren, other passersby, and friends.

Each June, the Lamberts host several work campers, Belle awakening us at 6 A.M. with steaming mugs of coffee, the aroma of freshly baked biscuits filling the house. In a crystal dish jelly waits to be spread with a sterling silver knife. At day's end, we return to find

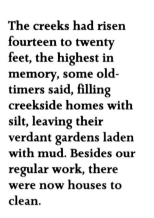

The creeks had risen fourteen to twenty feet, the highest in memory, some old-timers said, filling creekside homes with silt, leaving their verdant gardens laden with mud. Besides our regular work, there were now houses to clean.

our laundry done and fresh towels laid out in the bath.

Although Ben long ago left law enforcement, his influence lingers. At one work camp, I heard gunshots ring out close by in the night. Soon there was the clomp of boots on the porch, a knock at the door, the creak of stairs as Ben descended from above, then the sounds of muffled voices. At breakfast, Ben told us a man with a grudge had shot through a window at Ben's renter next door. The renter knew he had better tell Ben just as he knew he had better clear out by morning.

*B*en's is a solid, reassuring, protecting presence. His phone rings year round, and his answers are good deeds done throughout the county. During work camp, the Lamberts's kitchen is a busy nerve center, Belle fielding calls as Ben's expertise is needed here then there. But I never dreamed that through a stark predicament I would feel his love's long reach myself.

On a work-camp foray one year, Ben introduced me to Jackson Ridge, a beautiful ridge line along a mountain's top where an occasional leafy vista reveals the valley falling below. I thought it began as Jackson Branch, a dirt road that leaves the blacktopped main county road eight miles north of the chapel and winds up and up past rustic houses, flourishing gardens, small, rural churches. I thought, too, that it then wound circuitously down, ending its long, half-moon route at the main road again, south of the chapel.

One June when I was scheduled to deliver supplies with Ben, the county was hit with a devastating flood the day before we arrived. Plans abruptly changed. The creeks had risen fourteen to twenty feet, the highest in memory, some old-timers said, filling creekside homes with silt, leaving their verdant gardens laden with mud. Besides our regular work, there were now houses to clean.

Our days passed with crews toiling from Laurel Creek, an hour's drive from the chapel, to nearby Jehovah's Fork. Besides working temporarily at some sites, I drove many mountain miles, taking crews from site to site, always alert for the loaded coal trucks that notoriously hogged the narrow roads. Occasionally, my car would pass Ben's truck and we'd wave, or our paths would cross at the chapel as we picked up and dropped off tools. In the evenings, Ben would sink exhausted into a living room chair and instantly fall asleep.

By Thursday, we were all tired. That morning, I drove the crew of a teacher named Patsy—also from Atlanta and also staying at the Lamberts'—to a site at Jackson Branch. I stayed to help dig a new sewer line so we could lay PVC pipes. After finishing in late afternoon, most crew members opted to return to camp headquarters to swim, but Patsy and a teenager named Scott said they would accompany me to Jackson Ridge to see the sights.

As we ascended farther up Jackson Branch, I pointed out houses where Ben and I had dropped off supplies other years and where crews had built porches, repainted tin roofs, and dug holes for new outhouses. I never once thought about the flood rains, never once realized they could have affected the heights.

Starting down on the mountain's other side, we no longer passed houses, the dirt road growing progressively rocky and the forest lonely and wild. I didn't like it but thought it was just an unusual rough stretch and would soon straighten out. I was wrong. Stopping farther down so Scott could scout around a bend, I then resumed driving because he said it seemed to flatten out. But the smooth patch would prove short-lived and the road more menacing. My innocence gave way to alarm.

Steering that road was like shooting whitewater rapids, the deluge having stripped away the evenness, exposing raw, boulder shoals. I was driving into a trap, quickly reaching a point of no return, where backing up was as impossible as going ahead. Climbing exhausted from the car, I prayed, *Please, Lord, send help!*

I didn't know then that the road led deeper into wilderness, ending at a lake, and was checked only rarely by a conservation truck. Nor did I know that Jackson Branch and Jackson Ridge were actually parts of two separate roads that never met. I did know that we weren't in mortal danger. We *could* trek the long distance back to the ridge top to find a phone—except we were so tired from that hot day's digging. I wished I could call Ben. *He'd get us out!* I thought. Then I remem-bered he and Belle were away for the day.

"We have to turn around and go back up," said Patsy. "I'll be your right tire, Scott the left. Follow exactly where we lead." But it was mighty slow going as they strode ahead, manipulating my car inch by heaving inch to save its undercarriage.

Suddenly, in answer to my prayer, a four-wheel drive, half-ton truck appeared over the top of the hill, driving toward us. Its open back held hunting dogs, and in its cab were a man and boy going camping. Patsy explained our problem, and the stranger pulled his truck next to my car window. "You want me to drive that car outta here for you, ma'am?" he asked—an easier task for this hardy mountain man.

I thanked him afterwards, explaining we were work campers living at the Lamberts'. Then I asked if by some chance he knew Ben?

"Sure do!" he said, smiling broadly. "Why, he hauled *my* car out of a scrape worse'n this a long time ago. He's saved me *twice*, as a matter of fact!"

Just like Ben Lambert, a big man in every way. That saving bread he'd once cast upon the waters had now been returned by this stranger's love.

Ben Lambert manifests the strength of these mountains as Belle reflects their majesty. Individually and together, they have nurtured the land, the animals, and the people. And they have nurtured each other. One day I heard Belle tell Ben she was leaving the house to do some errands, and she asked if there was anything she could do for him while she was out.

"Just hurry back," he said.

Ben Lambert manifests the strength of these mountains as Belle reflects their majesty.

"Trigger, you seemed to be staring at me the first day we met," I said. "Yeah," he replied. "It was the love. I just knew you was my sister. I shook hands with you, and I hadn't felt love like that since Granddaddy."

7

Trigger John: "The Best of the Bunch"

Let mutual love continue. Do not neglect to show hospitality to strangers, for by doing that some have entertained angels without knowing it.
HEBREWS 13:1-2

*T*he only thing I knew at first was that I was frightened of Trigger John. He had the wildest eyes I'd ever seen, and they were focused right on me.

It was impossible not to spot him standing there in Squirrelly Dyer's yard, dressed in a bright-red shirt and speaking at the top of his voice. There was something so primal, so unpredictable about him—like a boar in the wild, preparing to attack. I intended to avoid this stocky, thirty-one-year-old mountaineer and stick as close to Arthur Thomas as I could. Arthur, my crew coleader at my fifth work camp, was a man I'd trust anywhere.

In 1979 work camp was still held in its original county, the one where Rev. Bob Bondurant had his rural church, and where most

Our crew set off, eagerly bouncing down the corduroy ruts of a mountain road, looking for Mayme Cluter's place. What awaited was desolation.

the moment we met. I'd lucked out, too, having as my coleader Arthur, a retired coal miner, work-camp veteran, and excellent carpenter. County-born sixty-four years before, he lived deep in a holler on 180 acres, hand-crafting knives and caning the seats of chairs with hickory bark he stripped from trees.

Assembling with all crew leaders on Monday, Arthur and I got two sites to complete—and an excellent crew: Massachusetts teenagers Kristin and Paul; county native Tina, age fifteen; fifteen-year-old Alex, an apprentice carpenter from Florida; and twenty-year-old Julie, another Floridian, and a work-camp veteran just back from study abroad. Our crew set off, eagerly bouncing down the corduroy ruts of a mountain road, looking for Mayme Cluter's place.

What awaited was desolation.

An old, dead tree with a few withered leaves stood to the left of the house with an angry, spotted dog chained nearby. Another dog, shackled to a rusty-car-hood shelter, barked fiercely next to him. Cacophony arose behind the house: chickens cackling and three more dogs, straining at chains and howling like the hounds of hell.

A brooding pall overhung the filthy, ram-

meetings were held at the county high school. I knew from the start this work camp would be memorable.

I'd been assigned to live in the tasteful trailer of Dasha Henderson, a divorced woman in her early thirties, who was the art teacher at the high school. We were friends

shackle house. Beyond the back porch piled with debris were an outhouse and rubbish heap rank with decay.

Inside the house, Mayme Cluter lay slowly dying, a toothless fifty pounds of yellow skin, eyes dark-rimmed in deep sockets. Emphysema fettered her to a sofa, plastic oxygen tubes in her nose extending to a machine that pumped night and day. Delbert, her husband of forty years, cared for her. He had a grizzled face and a huge stomach, and he walked with a cane, dragging his right leg paralyzed by a stroke several years before.

Thirty-year-old twin sons lived with them,

We analyzed what we'd do when materials arrived: put on a new roof; rebuild the back porch; rebuild and elongate the front porch.

The young women and I began to clean, hauling water from a muddy creek that meandered through the yard. Full of silt, the water needed boiling before dishes could be done.

watching a flickering TV all day and at night sleeping on greasy mattresses in anterooms piled with junk. Because Mayme and Delbert were cousins, it was said that these sons weren't bright.

Our site hadn't yet been supplied, so we analyzed what we'd do when materials arrived: put on a new roof; rebuild the back porch; rebuild and elongate the front porch. And there was an incredibly dirty kitchen to be cleaned: sooty walls, piled dishes thick with lard, and a refrigerator ice-coated outside, with fungus and a few eggs inside.

While Arthur measured for wood, the young women and I began to clean, hauling water from a muddy creek that meandered through the yard. Full of silt, the water needed boiling before dishes could be done. Pulling bags of chicken feed from under a table in order to sweep, Tina disgustedly crumpled her face.

What had once been potatoes was now a black-fungus pile.

The young men made a grim discovery, too. Clearing off the back porch, they shoved an old, metal stove, not knowing a hen had hatched her brood beneath. A chick they accidentally beheaded plus the stench of rotten eggs sent the nauseated crew members fleeing.

Delbert remained cheerful amidst all this as he settled in a chair by the open back door. Sun slanting across his belly, he told us how a man had let them live here free ever since their house down the road had fallen in.

I considered the peeling walls, collapsing ceiling, the foot-high hole in the kitchen door letting bees trespass in summer, frigid air in winter. *Live?* I thought. I pictured Mayme on the sofa that she couldn't leave, dignified and gasping, thanking us in hillbilly tones for coming here to help. We would try to ease her remaining days, bringing briefly to life the ridiculous motto framed above her head: Have a Lovely Day.

Work campers congregated each morning at Bob Bondurant's church to trade stories, pick up tools, and hitch rides to sites spread the county's length. But Tuesday morning, it was cleaning supplies I had in tow, having bought everything we needed to do a thorough job. And since we'd seen only eggs, beans, and Delbert's pan bread at the Cluters, I also had fresh fruit for them and a new coffee pot. At Dasha's, I had filled the coffee pot with water and fresh-ground coffee, which I'd later brew on Mayme's stove. It would accompany a casserole Kristin had cooked.

As coffee perked, sharing the stove with kettles of water kept aboil, we women sterilized and scoured the sink and washed cabinets, checking with Delbert before throwing anything out. He had defrosted the refrigerator overnight, and that helped. Mayme, asleep with her head back, mouth open, had endured a bad night. A thunderstorm had leaked rain through the roof, and the humidity made it hard to breathe.

Arthur took the young men to a sawmill, returning only to drop lumber off and pick us up, for we were scheduled to finish the morning at a place dear to him.

Arthur's character announced itself, and that character was rooted in faith. It had blossomed as a boy and was indestructible by the time he was a medic in World War II. It would later descend with him into the coal mines

Tuesday morning, it was cleaning supplies I had in tow, having bought everything we needed to do a thorough job. With kettles of water kept aboil, we women sterilized and scoured the sink and washed cabinets, checking with Delbert before throwing anything out.

and sustain him and his gentle wife, Eva, as they raised three daughters and a son.

That faith was simple: there was God, and there was Satan; and one's duty was "to bring other souls to Christ"—not that Arthur talked about it much. He lived his beliefs, treating every person who crossed his path like the good Lord himself. Arthur's goodness shone like the twinkling fireflies that filled his holler.

I wasn't surprised upon leaving Mayme's the day before when Arthur showed us the core of his life—a small, white church in a sun-splintered glen. Nor was I surprised when he asked us to attend his Tuesday morning prayer group that met in rural homes. Unlike the moderate religious services at camp, I knew this would be emotional.

What I didn't know about was Trigger.

*T*rigger's eyes riveted on me from the moment we arrived. Feeling threatened, I stayed by Arthur's side as we all packed into Squirrelly Dyer's small house.

I watched as simple folk, faces lined with care, sang hymns, gave testimonies, and embraced each speaker as troubles were revealed. The atmosphere intensified, one hour turning to two, the air growing stifling then smotheringly hot. The scene seemed almost surrealistic when everyone formed a circle, eyes closed, each one praying loudly and all at the same time. I felt suddenly dizzy, like I was bobbing along on a babbling sea of prayer, and wanted to scream, "Let me out!" But there was Trigger, blocking the doorway, eyes boring into me when he wasn't crying hysterically or shouting, *"Praise the Lord!"*

I felt relieved afterwards when we spilled out into the yard, but revulsion followed when Trigger came over to be introduced. Not wanting to touch this stranger who seemed so raw and uncivilized, so out of control, I very cooly shook hands, dropping mine as fast as I could.

It was a definite relief to get back to Mayme's, where I could forget him for a while and chat with Delbert on the rickety front porch. Although dressed in the same dirty clothes of the day before, there was something almost piquant about this former logger, who, with Mayme, had raised ten children. He produced a small chest, its hinges broken like everything else in this house, to show me faded family photographs. Even in her prime Mayme had looked thin. And since falling ill, she had lain uncomplaining, occasionally spitting into an ever-present cup.

Later that night, however, thoughts of Trigger came tumbling back as I made a journal entry:

I was frightened today by a wild-eyed character called Trigger John. Raised with his brothers and sisters way back in the woods, he said he'd always been afraid of women until he 'found the Lord.' He watched me constantly, needs a shave, talks loud, and says he's coming to our job tomorrow. I hope he doesn't!

But he did.

*A*s Arthur's truck pulled into Mayme's the next day, I stiffened. "Oh, he's *here!*" I said to Julie, sitting beside me. She'd had the same reservations about Trigger as I. Now there he stood by a truck of his own, hands on his hips, smiling ear to ear.

It was all I needed after a terrible night: head stuffy with an oncoming cold, left arm swollen from black fly bites, fretful sleep punctuated by a nightmare about birds I had to flee, and a pounding headache upon waking up.

I kept out of Trigger's way as the young women and I washed kitchen walls, aware I

I pictured Mayme on the sofa that she couldn't leave, dignified and gasping, thanking us in hillbilly tones for coming here to help. We would try to ease her remaining days, bringing briefly to life the ridiculous motto framed above her head: Have a Lovely Day.

So far, we'd almost completed the back porch, built the new front porch, put in some windows, washed the kitchen floor as our last task in there, and presented Mayme with a wildflower bouquet.

was *here* and he was *there*, helping Arthur and the young men. There was separation later, lunching in a holler, Trigger sitting apart.

With soft breezes and the sky a cornflower blue, it was a perfect summer day to sink into sweet-smelling, new-mown hay. What good workers our crew members were! I thought of Julie, a "people person," spending every spare moment she could with Mayme; and Tina, shy but opening out, so organized in her work. Strong, sensitive Kristin could look at anything; it was she who had helped me sweep up the decapitated chick. Alex was already accomplished with the tools, and Paul was hammering hard despite sunburn and obnoxious bees.

So far, we'd almost completed the back porch, built the new front porch, put in some windows, washed the kitchen floor as our last task in there, and presented Mayme with a wildflower bouquet.

And for me, mid afternoon would present a turning point.

*A*rthur's wife, Eva, brought a watermelon to our site, and we sat under trees across the road from Cluters', eating its succulent slices. Trigger, leaning back against a tree, began to talk.

He'd only gone as far as sixth grade in school, he said, and had only learned to sew. Partly, that was because he was afraid of women. His daddy had taught him that women were evil, so when his teachers were female, he'd been too scared to talk. His folks kept the family isolated from other kids, and it was only years later, after "being saved," that he realized the stories were false.

Then other things came out. Only able to read and write his name, he'd studied for a driver's license by listening as someone else read the information aloud. When officials tested him orally, he'd scored 100 percent.

Two-and-a-half years earlier, he said, his daddy had kicked him out, and ever since, he'd had no home. My attention arrested, I asked where he lived.

"In my truck," he replied.

And where did he sleep?

"In the truck. I just drive aroun' till I git tired then pull off somewheres by the side of the road."

And where did he bathe?

"In a crik. I drive down the road where there's no people, 'n take a towel and soap."

But what about in winter?

"I stop at a friend's house, and if they say no, just drive somewheres till someone says yes."

His blue, one-ton flatbed was his lifeline. So was an old school bus he owned, which he'd rigged with a stove. Sometimes he slept there. When I commented that he must be cold in winter, he answered without self-pity, "I've gotten along."

My sympathy aroused—but with only a tentative trust—I offered to teach him the alphabet. Fetching my journal from Arthur's truck, I sat down beside him and laid the letters out. Paul, I noticed, had photographed us.

"That's the first time I ever had my pitcher took with a woman," Trigger said.

And then I printed the words he'd shouted so frighteningly the day before: PRAISE THE LORD.

I wanted to share all this at dinner, but Dasha was away. I stood alone by the stove, my astonishment unallayed. How I'd misjudged Trigger! I felt like the Ancient Mariner when he

Fetching my journal from Arthur's truck, I sat down beside him and laid the letters out. I printed the words he'd shouted so frighteningly the day before: PRAISE THE LORD.

blessed the water snakes and his albatross fell away. This man, with all these obstacles, was making his life *work*—and all because of faith. He talked loud, sang loud, worked hard—all "for the Lord."

I remembered him bowing his head at lunch, saying a solitary grace. I remembered hearing him say, when he'd missed a nail and hammered his thumb, "Thank you, Lord, that didn't hurt too much!" I was *glad* now for his prayer group—the only real family he had. Then I remembered Arthur's words as we had driven from the site: of all the people in Trigger John's bloodline he was "the best of the bunch."

As I sat singing at the high school that night, my mind nearly numb from his impact, I became aware of Julie standing at my side.

Smiling sweetly, she reached down and took my hand. "It's nothing," she said. "I just wanted to touch you." Her hand was as clammy as mine, for Julie was the only one of the crew who realized the profundity of what we were experiencing.

"You know why Trigger's daddy run him off?" Arthur asked me on Thursday. "Because one Sunday, Trigger wanted to visit his granddaddy's grave, and his father wanted him to work. All that boy's ever known is work!"

His granddad was the only one who had ever really loved Trigger. Granddad had named him the night of his birth. Walking up a hill to Trigger's mother's house, he'd put a hand into one pocket, and when his fingers curled around his gun, his thumb was on the trigger.

Granddaddy was religious and prayed unceasingly that Trigger "be saved." Church, however, was full of women, and Trigger was afraid to attend. But one Sunday, when "it was rainin' an old, cold rain," he'd somehow entered its door. "You couldn't 'a gotten no further back in the church," he said, "and I seen the women sittin' there. But somethin' give me courage to march to the front." He couldn't remember what happened next—so transported had he been—but he knew without doubt his soul had been cleansed. "I was up next day before daylight, done my feedin', and went to tell Granddad the good news."

Salvation changed his life. "You wouldn't 'a knowed me before I started living for God. I didn't tease nobody, and if anybody 'a teased me, he'd 'a had a fist to his head. Now I say, 'I'll pray fer you' and walk away. When you're a sinner, you cuss about somethin'—oh, man, I used to done as much of it as the next man— but when you're saved, you laugh about it. That way, the devil don't git the victory."

Trigger rededicated the title of his truck "to the Lord" and then repaid an old, gnawing debt. His family was known locally as the "Spot and Steal Gang." "If you stole it, you buried it. Then after the law cooled down, you dug it up and used it." But Trigger had only stolen twice. One item was a flashlight, and in contrition, he launched a year-long search for its owner. Finally finding the owner in a crowded post office, Trigger announced, "Clyde Ferguson, I got a 'fession to make!" And he was instantly forgiven.

Trigger paid his whole debt to Granddad, too. After salvation, Trigger became janitor of his small, country church, giving it up when Granddad got sick. For a year and a half, he fed and nursed his dying kin, carrying him bodily whenever the need arose. And when Granddad was gone, he left Trigger a legacy: his Bible, his flashlight—and his love.

I learned much more about Trigger's character and grace on Thursday, too. When we got to the Cluters' in Arthur's truck, he politely opened my door. And when I went up to photograph the crew on the roof, he appeared at the top of the ladder to hold it secure. When I went up again to help with tar paper, it was he who handed me nails and also let me use his mattock.

"You're the first woman I've ever roofed with," he said.

As we hammered, he said he had a birthday coming up—"my birthday in the Lord. It's six years since I became a Christian."

"Six years old, Trigger, is when people learn to read," I said.

Arthur drove us to a little park for lunch, Trigger spreading out the picnic he'd brought along to share. He'd also brought me a gift, purchased at a yard sale as he'd driven that morning to the site. "Hope you don't mind," he said. I immediately donned the dark-green jacket of a former jacket-dress, its 20¢ price tag still attached.

Julie gave him a gift as well: a notebook all his own. Earlier, Trigger had excitedly shown the journal page of the day before, and he said of the homework he'd done overnight, "I just got this paper clear full!"

Sitting there, I taught him the vowels, then printed the sentence: My name is John.

Friday we adventured with Arthur after first finishing up at the Cluters. We'd arrived there at nine—me serving them coffee as I did every day, Arthur constructing a set of front steps, and the crew caulking the chimney to stop a leak. Then after we filed into the living room to bid a grateful Mayme good-bye and after I had photographed the delighted Delbert on the new front porch with the crew, we said our final "God bless you!" and left.

We traveled for miles, Arthur passing Salt Lick, a watering hole for deer, where his great-granddaddy once used to hunt. One day, he said, great-granddaddy's dog growled, warning him just in time of the mountain lion set to spring.

We spent the afternoon at open bogs nestled in a natural bowl at 3400 feet. A geologic mystery in those Southern mountains, it resembled an arctic tundra filled with rare plants, birds, mammals, and moss that belonged much farther north. Walking the boardwalk that wound through the bogs, we stopped to read the signs. I'd begun to teach Trigger something of phonetics, and he patiently sounded out words.

There was a swirling square dance at the high school that night. "Heel-toe, heel-toe,

Friday we adventured with Arthur. We spent the afternoon at open bogs nestled in a natural bowl at 3400 feet. A geologic mystery in those Southern mountains, it resembled an arctic tundra filled with rare plants, birds, mammals, and moss that belonged much farther north.

slide-step-slide," taught the hillbilly caller, the young women swaying like flowers in a field, the young men bowing with bright, cheerful smiles.

Meanwhile, in me an awe was growing—for the force of the human spirit, once it has been claimed by God.

*S*aturday morning I went to the laundromat and ran right into Trigger. "I didn't know what caused me to go there that mornin'," he said later on, "but I knew after I seen you what it was. I prayed so hard for the Lord to send someone to help me with readin'."

For three years in my New England town, I'd been an aide in a learning disabilities class and had learned to take language apart. Now Trigger and I sat on a wall outside, sharing a lesson while our laundry washed. His notebook was with him; he'd been practicing his words. "When you git back to Massachusetts, you can say you met a hillbilly that didn't know nothin' but now knows a *lot*!"

"I got somethin' fer you," he said when we were through. Reaching into his truck with a grin and a flourish, he extracted and held up a gift.

A huge apple for his teacher!

Trigger also appeared unexpectedly at Bob Bondurant's church on Sunday. I invited him to adult Sunday school, where, together, we read the Scripture lesson aloud, me stopping to let him read words he now knew by sight. At the later church service he said he'd been nervous, " 'cause I ain't never done anythin' like it before. But I was proud of myself, fer as *that* goes. . . ."

*T*rigger John had every reason to be proud; he'd worked faithfully all of his life. As a child, his nine brothers and sisters had lazily watched, taunting him as he toiled. Turned down by the army, he'd swept out his church; but after Granddad's death, he had "gotten the greenback" for hauling trash, carpentry work, and digging occasional graves.

Merchants trusted him and extended credit—once for the only new pants he'd ever had. "There was gonna be a revival at church, and I thought, *I'm not gonna wear old clothes. I'm gonna buy me a pair of pants!* I went to Mrs. Leslie's store—already owed her thirteen dollars for a jacket—and she said, 'You sure you want to pay this much?' Well, they was blue and nice, and I said, 'Yes, ma'am.' They was ten-somethin' with the tax, and I still owe

Beginning our second site, we found Janet Boggs's trailer home set deep in shade that exactly matched her mood. We were to underpin her trailer then build an outhouse and porch.

her for 'em. When I go in this month, I don't know which bill she'll jerk out—the jacket or pants!"

Mostly, though, he wore yard-sale clothes but didn't know his size. "I just take my arm and measure down to the end of my fingers. Then I know if the pants will fit."

Trigger depended on himself, whether dining alone—"I 'et my supper in White Oak Holler last night: beans, radishes, Kool-Aid"—or sleeping in his truck at various locales. He filled his leisure by "sometimes on Sundays goin' through two tanks of gas, runnin' around the countryside, lookin' at God's creation, not what man's created." He wanted "to get where I wasn't disturbin' people a whole lot," he said.

Sometimes, though, others perceived his needs. "One day, I spent my last two dollars on gas . . . just enough to git me to revival," Trigger said. "After the service, a man—I ain't gonna name no names—gave me a twenty-

Arthur was imaginative about lunch sites, and Monday's was a railroad station long since closed down. We sat on the track, eating watermelon he sliced, and "friendship cake" Eva had sent.

dollar bill. 'John,' he said, 'the Lord laid it on my heart to give you this.'"

*T*he next week, beginning our second site, we found Janet Boggs's trailer home set deep in shade that exactly matched her mood. At twenty-nine, she was divorced, defeated, and four weeks earlier she had delivered her third child. The husband who had fathered her first two children, now nine and five, had disappeared in the middle of one night and simply never returned. The father of the newest child had also taken off. We were to underpin her trailer then build an outhouse and porch.

Janet's father lived in a house next door and dressed dandily, but it was his cruelty we saw. He hadn't spoken to his daughter since the baby's birth. And although he let her children bathe in his tub, it was a privilege she was denied.

We hoped to reconcile them before we left.

Janet's trailer was depressing—and dangerous. The bathroom, useless because it had no water line, was filled with damp clothes she hadn't yet hung. And there was an appalling smell of gas from kitchen stove jets, their blue flames burning to dispel the chill. She lived on a small welfare check, not nearly enough to buy clothes for her children.

As we worked, we wove Janet in until she was part of the crew. She'd only gone to tenth grade in school and regretted that she'd left. Intrigued by my lessons with Trigger, she was amused on Monday when he took his first "test."

Arthur was imaginative about lunch sites, and Monday's was a railroad station long since closed down. We sat on the track, eating watermelon he sliced, and "friendship cake" Eva had sent. Trigger, captivated by our square dance recollections, thought he'd like to learn some steps. So we all passed a light-hearted hour, clapping, do-si-doing, and swinging arm in arm.

"You're the first woman I've ever danced with," Trigger said.

Returning from lunch, Trigger told me it hurt him to think of our leaving.

Had he ever thought of returning home, I asked.

Trigger, captivated by our square dance recollections, thought he'd like to learn some steps. So we all passed a light-hearted hour, clapping, do-si-doing, and swinging arm in arm. Returning from lunch, Trigger told me it hurt him to think of our leaving.

"Yeah, if it was a peaceable place," he said. "I done went back three times and tried, but them brothers of mine just don't let it work. I love my people, but they don't want to socialate with me. They don't want me to learn nothin', 'n do everything against me they can. The Lord laid it on my heart to flee. My fightin' days is over . . . I'm gonna live in peace. And

God's gonna provide some land of my own someday. He's answered one prayer, and he's gonna answer another . . . but he'll answer it in his *own* way."

"You've got patience, John," I said softly.

*T*rigger's sadness deepened each day.

On Tuesday, as I sat resting on a rock in the sun, Julie said, "I never saw a look on his face like that."

Trigger was sitting on a lumber pile, quietly looking down.

"Are you sad, John?" I asked.

"Somethin' like that," he said.

He'd mentioned once that he'd never had a girlfriend but hadn't felt lonesome. Now, as I moved beside him, putting my arm around his shoulders, he said, "Lonesome is gonna be when you leave. You're more like a mother than I ever had. I can't tell you fellers what you mean to me . . . can't seem to find the words. But I found out when Granddad died, that God would hold me up. I 'spect I'd 'a torn the place upside down, but I'd been saved two years and a half before. I have Jesus—and that means the whole world to me."

"Trigger, through education, another world will open up to you, too," I said.

Our lessons continued: the long and short vowel sounds and the "Magic E Rule" that turned *pal* to *pale* and *sit* to *site*. We sat on woodpiles, on heaped-up dirt by the new outhouse hole, along country lanes at lunchtime— his mind filling, while his teacher was also being taught. Janet encouraged him, their friendship budding all the while. "When I started out, the only thing I could read was my name," he told her. "Now I can read a lot."

He told her, too, how his mother had scorned him when he'd taken his test paper to show her on Monday night. I'd had him write the sentence: THIS IS AN ANGEL.

"Angels isn't on paper; they's in heaven," she had said with a smirk.

"They call me the dummy of the bunch," Trigger said.

"You're the smartest of the bunch," Janet replied.

One morning, when we arrived at church to hitch our ride with Arthur, Trigger was already there, truck heaped with wood. We had all donated money to buy Janet a coal/wood stove, which Arthur would install when we left.

As we piled the oak and poplar at Janet's,

Trigger said, "She needs help, and I'm gonna take care of her till the right man comes along."

Her father had also gotten into the act after observing the respect and affection in which we held Janet and the joy we took in her children. When Janet's father meandered over one day, dressed like a "dude" in white pants, suspenders, black shirt, and hat, Arthur had told him diplomatically that his conduct toward his daughter was disgraceful. The father promised to make amends.

At our last day's lesson, Trigger said a friend's wife had offered to teach his lessons during the summer. I encouraged him also to continue in the fall through an evening program at the high school. We spoke of our mutual sadness at parting, too, but I told him that God never closed one door without opening another. It was then he said he loved me nearly as much as Granddaddy, "though no one could ever take *his* place."

"Trigger, you seemed to be staring at me the first day we met," I said.

"Yeah," he replied. "It was the love. I just knew you was my sister. I shook hands with you, and I hadn't felt love like that since Granddaddy."

Trigger got there early, pressing a note—the first he'd ever written—into my hand when I arrived. JESUS AND JHN LOVES YOU, it said.

"What was your granddaddy's name?" I asked.

"Frank Carpenter," he replied.

I pulled my breath in, struck by a stunning coincidence. My grammar school principal in Massachusetts—where I'd learned to read at age six—had ironically been a man named Carpenter!

Work camp closed with a candle-lit communion service in the high school auditorium. Trigger got there early, pressing a note—the first he'd ever written—into my hand when I arrived.

JESUS AND JHN LOVES YOU, it said.

Crews sat in circles on the floor, guests in chairs along the auditorium's walls, while communion service participants, including me—I was to read the Scripture—sat by the stage in the front of the hall. There was a "sharing time," when, if they wished, the young people and the adults could rise, one at a time, and tell what work camp had meant to them. While candles flickered, I stood and shared some bittersweet thoughts.

"Each work camp year, I've been impressed by something different: the first year, poverty; to be superceded other years by Appalachian generosity, the sheer beauty of this place, family relationships. So I was curious what this year's emphasis would be. I've discovered it's hellos and good-byes."

I told of meeting Trigger, how I'd taught him the rudiments of reading while learning much more from this man who "tried to be the same in the world as in the church." I spoke of his melancholy at our leaving—but that life was not a void—and how one day, as we'd driven from Janet Boggs's site, Trigger had waved good-bye to us from Janet's living room, where he sat rocking her baby.

Trigger, sitting against the wall with Eva Thomas, started to cry then bent forward, his face covered with his hands. Unexpectedly, he jumped up. "I just *knowed* Sister Nancy was sent!" he cried passionately. "And come October, I'm gonna be in this here *school!*"

Eva threw her arms up, palms turned toward heaven. *"Praise the Lord!"* she exclaimed.

I saw Trigger once more that evening. After the service, I filled a van with work campers and drove five miles to an ice-cream stand. I didn't want any, so I sat waiting for them, windows open to the fragrant, summer air.

Suddenly, Trigger was standing by the driver's side window. "I figgered you'd be here," he said. "I want to buy you ice cream."

I already knew I was the first woman for whom he'd ever bought ice cream.

When he returned, he passed the cone in with his left hand, resting his right on the van windowsill. I looked for the last time into the eyes of this good man who didn't know his own goodness, this happy man who'd never once thought abstractly about happiness, this untutored genius in the art of living.

Then I bent my head and kissed the hand that had known only work.

> **I looked for the last time into the eyes of this good man who didn't know his own goodness . . . this untutored genius in the art of living.**

We discovered that educational backgrounds
didn't matter nor did economic
circumstances. For both Appalachians and
work campers, love mattered. That was all.
We bonded like chemical atoms in
relationships of sincerity and trust.

EPILOGUE

I was glad when they said to me, "Let us go to the house of the Lord!"
PSALM 122:1

*M*y purpose in this book wasn't to write a sociological treatise about Appalachia but simply to describe what I and others saw and felt during our work-camp experiences. We discovered that educational backgrounds didn't matter nor did economic circumstances. For both Appalachians and work campers, love mattered. That was all. We bonded like chemical atoms in relationships of sincerity and trust.

To uphold that trust of these dear Appalachian friends who allowed me to tell their stories, and to honor their privacy, I changed the names of certain people as well as locales and left the counties unidentified. The fictitious names, however, are common throughout the area.

I never saw the "three Appalachian women" again, yet their impacts remain. Last year, I did talk by phone with Lula McCoy—still earth-mothering a brood now expanded by many grandchildren.

I never saw Trigger again, either. But I subscribed to his county's newspaper and learned that God did provide an answer to his second prayer. Four years after we'd worked together, I saw this announcement:

> Mr. and Mrs. Charley Cutlip announce the forthcoming marriage of their daughter, Crystal Ann, to Trigger John Carpenter, son of Mr. and Mrs. William Carpenter. The couple will exchange their vows on October 20, 1983 at 1:00 P.M. at the Upper Branch Church in Valley View. It will be an open church wedding and everyone is welcome.

So Trigger now had a family and land of his own.

Hallie Hamrick and I have never lost touch, corresponding all through the years. She came to visit us once in Massachusetts, in a group that also included Rev. Bob Bondurant, Dasha Henderson, and Arthur Thomas. I'd written about her in our local newspaper, and she was greeted with enthusiasm all over town, enchanting everyone she met. She eventually continued her education, earning a high-school-equivalency diploma, thus fulfilling a long-cherished dream. Her grandson, David, graduated from high school and lives and works in Virginia.

Shayne is sixteen now, a budding artist who's taking the college preparatory course, hopefully to pursue higher education upon high school graduation. I shall watch his progress through life while continuing to love him from the depths of my heart.

The Duke and Duchess are busy as ever—Ben still involved in work camp, good deeds, and serving as an elder at the chapel, Belle recently completing a course on finances for women. Typically, she's been asked to teach the course next year.

As for the Adkinses and "the house where miracles met," Philip hasn't touched a drop of alcohol since the June we worked at his house. Because we had a well put in, a work-camp crew the following year installed a water line and bathroom. The summer after that, Philip added porches to the front and back of the house. And last June, he, Gail, and Wesley appeared at the chapel to help rebuild someone else's house.

In "my Father's house" there are indeed many mansions.